A Legend in Your Own Lunch Box

T. J. Abney

PAGE PUBLISHING, INC.
Conneaut Lake, PA

First originally published by Page Publishing 2021

ISBN 978-1-6624-4334-3 (pbk)
ISBN 978-1-6624-7469-9 (hc)
ISBN 978-1-6624-4335-0 (digital)

Printed in the United States of America

Acknowledgments

THIS BOOK IS dedicated to my friends, my chosen family, and many teachers and authors along the way who ignited a spark in me that led me to discover the path that I am now on and taught me many things about being true to myself and listening to my soul. Without these friends, soulmates, and teachers, this book wouldn't have been possible. You will hear me reference many of these people throughout my journey in the following pages, so I wanted to make sure I acknowledge all of them from the very beginning. Thanks so much for giving me wisdom beyond measure and the courage and confidence to take this journey. I love you all from my soul.

To all my friends and teachers around the world—some of whom I personally know and others whom I have come to know through their books, teachings, podcasts, and the examples and experiences they have all shared to enrich my life. I want to pass on my deepest thanks, appreciation, and admiration for all that you've done for me.

I would like to thank God. And to be very clear from the beginning, when I say God or reference God throughout this book, I'm not speaking of the limiting mental and religious construct that I was taught growing up. I truly believe that "God" (the creation force of the entire universe) lives within me, as me. He/she/they is, in fact, me. I've also learned that tapping into this creation force inside of me is the only thing I truly need to manifest the life that I want. I hope that one day, everyone can have their own personal and creative relationship with whatever or whomever they call "God" like the relationship that has developed for me.

Contents

Preface

You are being presented with a choice: evolve or repeat.

—Creig Crippen, *The Mind's Journal*

YOU'D HAVE TO be living under a rock to not notice that the world that we live in today is particularly out of whack and in need of some serious realignment. Turn on the news, pick up a newspaper, or listen to most people's conversations, and you will quickly know that so many things in our current state of being have gone askew. Countries are on edge. World leaders are poised with their fingers on the proverbial red button as the whisper or threat of monumental-wars-to-come circle the globe. The family unit continues to deteriorate. Religious groups are fighting against each other for their beliefs to be the dominant belief system. The plague of systemic and widespread racism and the senseless killing of so many people is a weekly occurrence. We hear stories of incredible neglect and abuse on a daily basis. Child and adult trafficking have become an infection on our planet with no cure in sight. We are collectively and systematically killing our planet, depleting our natural resources all for a faster, more convenient experience in our daily lives. We now live in a world of twenty-four-hour news, and if you are even slightly awake, you've probably asked yourself on more than one occasion: What is going on here?

In our own, much smaller, and seemingly insignificant circles, friends are betraying friends, families are breaking apart, people are climbing over each other in the pursuit of the ultimate success in life. The endless thirst for gossip and the eternal quest for instant gratification has led us to a place where many people on our planet are constantly screaming out, "It's all about *me, me, me!*"

Surprisingly, there is a fundamental truth hidden deep down in that last statement, but not in the way that most of us would imagine. In fact, your life is about *you*! And when you make it about your true *you*, you come to a place where it automatically becomes about other people and the world collectively. The Buddha said it best when he said, "The only way to bring peace to the earth is to learn to make our own life peaceful."

For a long time now, there has been a deep desire inside me to write my experiences and the lessons I learned down in the hopes that it would help other people navigate this crazy, wonderful, and beautiful thing called life. The idea of writing something that would help people was something that has, for a long time, been on my bucket list, but I never made time to actually commit to it. So, in essence, it was just a pipe dream; that all changed in December of 2017. It's at this time that I truly believe with every fiber of my being that God, the Universe, along with some other very dear friends of mine, gently watered that deeply seeded ambition inside me, and things came to life. Right before Christmas of that year, after having several very deep, gut-wrenchingly difficult and yet, in the end, uplifting conversations with those dear friends and with myself, I decided that I wanted and needed to change. After examining my past and, quite honestly, reliving parts of my past over and over for far too long, I understood that nothing in my life would change if I didn't change it. In short, I just wanted all the pain to *stop*! I wanted to *evolve* and stop *repeating*. So I decided on Christmas Eve of that same year to start a new journey, write this book, redirect my life, and most importantly, overhaul the entire belief system I'd held for decades.

Creig Crippen, from the opening quote at the top of the very first page, to me is a great thought leader from the University of Colorado, and it's true! You are constantly being presented with those two choices and those two choices only. What's it going to be? Do you want to *evolve* beyond your current situation and circumstances, or do you want to continue to *repeat* lessons you're just so tired of seeing become a reality in your life? Today, and every day ahead, you get to decide.

Creig went on to say the following. "If you choose to remain unchanged, you will be presented with the same challenges, the same routine, the same storms, and the same situations until you learn from them until you love yourself enough to say, *No more,* and until you choose change. If you choose to evolve, you will connect with the strength within you, you will explore what lies outside your comfort zone, you will awaken to love, and you will become, you will *be. You have everything you need. Choose to evolve. Choose love.*"

I am no expert on the cosmos, and I don't have a solid understanding of how God or the universe operates. I've learned I'm never going to understand everything about God, and quite frankly, I don't believe we are supposed to. I am, however, the expert in everything that you will find written in this book because it's my life, my experiences, and the lessons I've learned along the way. I truly believe that the spark inside one person can change the world. So now, imagine, the more people that start to awaken and change their current life experience, the more sparks we will all share in recreating our existence and our experience here on earth.

I imagine we all have parts of our past we wish we could forget. I thought it was best to forget as well for such a long time until I continually came face-to-face with the ghosts which have haunted my adulthood for far too long. Through that process, I've ultimately learned it's much better to confront your past and deal with all of it and then let it go, rather than continuing to suppress and sweep feelings under the rug of your life. That's why I'm so glad I started meditating.

Meditation for me has been a godsend. I've always looked up to people like Oprah Winfrey and Deepak Chopra because they are extraordinary teachers of life, and I identify with everything they teach because it resonates within my soul as coming from a true and divine place. I'm also an avid reader and will read just about anything I can get my hands on. In the last year, I've also become a lover of podcasts because they truly expand my mind and way of thinking. This book is a combination of things I've read, mentors that I've listened to, and experiences with friends and family. These things and those people have ultimately become some of my closest teachers on this journey and helped me to become who I am. "Who I am" and "who you are" is totally the point; it's your life, your experiences, and you already have everything you need inside of you to create any life that you want.

I now know that everything happens by design. Nothing is an accident. Maybe, picking up this book is absolutely what was supposed to happen in your life, and my highest hope is that it speaks to you in every way that you need and encourages you to start your own journey toward becoming the highest, grandest version of yourself.

More than ten years ago now, in a conversation with my dear friend Carl, I heard the expression "A legend in your own lunch box," and when I did, I somehow knew that it would become something very special one day. Carl is originally from New Zealand, and he explained to me that in his country, that expression meant that someone was full of themselves. I knew deep down, though, it didn't have to keep that connotation. Ultimately, it became the title of this, my first book, and I think it's just perfect. At the same time, something in my gut tells me that there will be many more books coming to form a sort of legend series.

That title may sound strange at first to most people because, after all, what's so special about a lunch box, you may say. Think about it like this, remember when you were a kid, and your mom or dad or grandmother or aunt, whoever raised you, either did it for you or helped you pack your lunch box for school. Maybe you still do the same thing today when you are preparing to head out to work or school. Regardless, there is something that I've come to recognize that is so beautiful in that process that applies to everything that you will find in the pages of this book. All I'm asking is that you try and visualize the connection that I've noticed to something seemingly so simple and how it applies to the life that you are creating for yourself this very day.

Like preparing your lunch box for the day ahead and the physical nutrition it will bring, you can and should do the same thing from a mental, emotional, and spiritual standpoint. If you want the absolute best day, then you need to prepare yourself for the thoughts you will allow into your mind, the emotions and behavior of others that you will allow into your heart, and the people and circumstances that you will allow access to your spirit. Once you take the time and develop the strong habit of preparing your "lunch box," I have seen firsthand the phenomenal things you can accomplish and the landscape that you can actively create for your life. That's ultimately what I would like to share with you here; my experience, relatable stories about friends that taught me something along the way, and some tools and techniques that have proven very effective for me in preparing for the day ahead that you might want to try. Just give it a go. See what changes. *I dare you*!

To be a legend in your own lunch box and in life involves dedication, *practice*, taking a very long look at yourself, and making the determined decision to change. It won't always be an easy road, but here's a truth that you can hold onto. Your life will improve exponentially! At least, for me, when my soul was practically screaming at me to wake up, I had no choice but to pay attention. For some divine reason, I've never forgotten the expression "A legend in your own lunch box," and, boy, I'm glad I didn't.

Now, in my lunch box, this book, I've packed the following snacks for each of us: meditation, intention, attention, satisfaction, decisiveness, detachment, gratitude, forgiveness, fearlessness, compassion, presence, and freedom because all of these things prepare me for the best day each and every day of my life.

First and foremost, I call upon every word of this book to hit its mark in your heart, soul, and mind for the world's highest good. I hope everyone will become a legend in life because when you truly work at it, the entire world is at your fingertips, and all your dreams are possible. In fact, you deserve it all!

Now, I want you to sit back, enjoy the view into my journey, and let's learn together how we can all become legends in life!

1

A Meditating Legend

Be still and know that I am God.

—God (Me)

I HAD A relatively normal upbringing. I've always been a hard worker and have always found it easy to set professional goals and achieve them. However, when it comes to setting goals for my personal, spiritual, and mental development, let's just say I used to suck at it; but I, like you, am a constant work in progress. I've come to accept that more and more now, but it took a lot to get to where I am today.

I've had a very busy professional life. Before deciding to follow my instinct and become a writer, I worked in the realm of professional beauty, more specifically hair care as an educator. The opportunities to travel the world were numerous, and I enjoyed every moment of those experiences. I have made lasting friendships all over the world that mean so much to me. In my previous role as an education leader, I was responsible for developing educational content and how it rolls out year after year for all of our education team members worldwide. I often joked that my house was just a fancy storage unit because I seldom spent a great amount of time at home. On average, I was on the road forty-five weeks out of every year, and the time I did have at home in my office was spent on administrative tasks and planning activities. Let's just say I was hard-pressed for free time. If I did manage to score a vacation, it was usually a "staycation" because I couldn't imagine spending time off on another airplane or in another hotel. Those of you out there that travel for work will understand completely. Striking a work-life balance proved to be a challenge most of my professional career. I can't begin to fathom if I had a family to support, kids that needed help with homework, etc. So kudos to the people reading this that have a family to care for in the midst of their busy work lives.

Honestly, the idea of extra time to rest, recharge, and recollect myself was not a luxury that I thought I would ever have. Being that I worked in such a highly creative field with even more highly creative people, I was constantly emptying my tank, so to speak, through teaching, inspiring, mentoring, and dealing with the occasional tough conversations and situations that came my way. I worked in a world where I didn't have the luxury of having a day off because I was on a platform to reach people, and I took that responsibility seriously. However, it was very daunting and virtually impossible to live up to when all I was doing was emptying myself on a daily basis and never having anything of much substance to fill my tank.

At the end of 2017, things truly started to boil over. I was constantly frustrated, angry, tired, and depressed, along with a litany of other emotions. What seemed like overnight, I was no longer being creative; I was just executing. I don't know how many of you have ever felt like that, but if you have, then you know it's not a good feeling. I was existing in a space where it seemed like everyone around me just wanted more and more and, guess what, even *more*! How did this happen? How did I get here? How did a job that I truly loved become such an overwhelming daily task? How could I switch it all back to a place of true enjoyment? I started to ask myself those questions over and over again and, at the same time, ask the universe, even God, because I was that desperate. What happened next was truly astonishing. That's right, *nothing happened*! This made me even more frustrated.

Where was God? Where was this benevolent universe I had read so many books about—the universe that, if you ask, you shall receive in direct proportion to your request and your intent? Did God not feel like hearing from me? Was I not important enough for God to respond? Here, I was finally giving God a chance to be a part of my life, and God was choosing silence. Of course, I had rarely made time for God, so what could I expect? Beyond my anger, speculation, doubt, and frustration, God did show up anyway.

Let me be clear, this wasn't anything like the experience of Neale Donald Walsch in the book series *Conversations with God*. I'm not sure I could have handled that just yet. I'm still not sure I could handle that today. For those of you that have read *Conversations with God* by Neale Donald Walsch, you will know exactly what I'm referring to. For those of you that haven't, I highly recommend reading his trilogy. It is, without a doubt, a series of writings that catapulted me into the experiences I am having today, and it has become a cornerstone of my faith and renewed my soul's belief that having a genuine, loving, and very real relationship with the universe and my purpose is truly possible. To this day, I find myself reading and rereading everything written in his books because it brings clarity, solace, and ultimately, a peace of mind and peace in my soul that I haven't been able to find anywhere else.

For me, the answers to my questions came much more subtly and in a combination of ways. I have come to know that the universe can and does speak to us in more ways than we can usually comprehend, or maybe, we just aren't ready to actively listen. It was during this time that I had some heartfelt conversations with my very dear friends Luis and Selina along with more soul searching, and it led me down the path to meditation, and I am oh so glad that it did.

Those closest to me know that I am a very overachieving person. If I put my mind to something, then watch out because I go at it with guns blazing and give it everything I've got. This was no different now that I had decided to become the *best meditator* in the world! Trust me, that's just who I am.

I have long been a fan of Elizabeth Gilbert's books, especially *Eat, Pray, Love,* and those of you that know the book or movie well, then I can tell you that my ideas surrounding meditation were almost identical to hers in the beginning. My first order of business was to clear out one of my spare bedrooms and renovate it into the best mediation chamber anyone had ever seen. I maxed out my credit card at Pier One Imports and World Market to acquire everything I would need to build my sanctuary. It was so easy, and I felt so good that the hardest part was over. How naive was I?

So now, I was ready for my first successful meditation. The night before, I made sure that I had the incense ready, the most tranquil music I could find, and a room full of candles. During the renovation, I had decided that the room should have an Indian design because that's the only people I knew of that meditated successfully. I had my statues of Ganesh and Buddha and Lakshmi set up along with a few framed pictures of Jesus, Archangel Michael, and Krishna. Trust me, I was totally set! Even as I write this, I can still hear my friend Selina laughing uncontrollably at my exuberance.

Finally, the first morning of meditation had come. I could barely contain my excitement. Trust me, that excitement didn't last long. I lit the candles and incense, started the music, sat down on my comfy floor cushions, closed my eyes, and just waited to transcend to another world and talk with God; this was going to be so easy! Let's just say what happened next was an epic fail. I kept waiting and waiting and *waiting* for something remarkable to happen, and the only thing I experienced was a flood of frustration and so many thoughts and questions jumping into my mind? What had I done wrong? Was it not the right incense? Was it too many candles? The music wasn't right? Yeah, that's it, it *must be* the music! That night, I tried to do it again for ten minutes. I had selected what I thought to be more peaceful music. Still, nothing happened. My next thought was that I had wasted so much time and money to make this experience perfect, and nothing happened. How could this be? I asked again. Again, no answer. I was so frustrated that I left the room, closed the door, and didn't even think about entering my luxurious "sanctuary" again for a long time.

A few weeks later, I was talking to my friend Selina about my first experience since she was one of the biggest advocates of meditation from the get-go—even she laughed a little at my naivety.

"What did you expect to happen on your first try?" she asked.

"I don't know. I just assumed that I would sit there, close my eyes, and something miraculous would happen. Maybe even some swirling lights or angels would appear," I said.

My answer made her laugh even more. Then, she shared some wisdom with me that I truly believe was also God answering my question through her. She suggested that I try guided meditation in the beginning to help me along and give me something to focus on. With some reluctance, I started researching to find the "best guided meditation" on the market, and I was led to Deepak Chopra and Oprah Winfrey. Thank God I found them!

This was a *completely* different experience for me from the very first session. *You should know I'm a huge fan of Oprah!* I think she is one of the most forward-thinking and thought-provoking teachers of our time; however, I didn't have any knowledge of Deepak Chopra. I knew his name, but not much else. Let me tell you that the combination of both of those influential spiritual leaders changed my meditation experience forever. They have been working together for some time now on creating these guided meditations and have so many different options on their websites on how to purchase and download them. The thing I like best about their guided meditations is that each one you select is a twenty-one-day meditation with a specific focus on many of the things you would want to meditate on anyway. Their programs are still my mediation of choice every morning.

With their help every morning, I have been encouraged to continue to explore my meditation practice, and that has led me to Kundalini mantras and transcendental meditation, and I am continually fascinated by all of the options that are available if I just make the time. This practice has unlocked a passion inside of me that I now know I will never be able to walk away from.

In my career, I have had so many amazing experiences and even more amazing teachers, and all of them have led me to a fundamental belief about myself. I am a teacher at heart. One of the best rewards for me, in being a teacher, is that I also get to learn along the way. At my core, I know that the responsibility of teaching others is so that you may offer encouragement, experience, and wisdom for your student to step into a higher level of themselves and, in turn, learn something more about yourself. The whole motivation behind being a good teacher, for me, is to inspire someone or many people to change their thoughts, actions, or behaviors around a thing; that's why I will always be a teacher. The feeling I get from teaching someone something and then watching the light bulb above their heads turn on is a feeling for me that I will never be able to buy, which makes it incredibly priceless. So I've asked myself: What can my experience with meditation teach you?

When sharing my experience and the things I have learned with anyone, I think it's crucial to be completely transparent and then let them make the decision on whether or not to apply it to their own lives. I know that honesty breeds trust, so here goes.

Right off the bat, let me state, rather emphatically and from arduous experience, that meditation is a *practice*. And much like many of the things you are great at in your life today, they took practice. Meditation is no different at all. The more you practice, the better the experience becomes. I would encourage anyone thinking about starting meditation to go into it with a completely open mind, figuratively and literally. Liken it to whatever comes to mind: learning to ride a bike, playing the piano, being great at cooking, or making clothing; it all takes practice, practice, and practice.

Becoming great in your meditation practice is a journey that will constantly change and grow. Again, the more you practice, the more your experience will grow and deepen. Let me be very clear, sometimes, you will experience great sensations of peace, lightheartedness, and joy, and then again, sometimes, it seems nothing has happened. All of this, and I do mean *all*, is completely normal and a part of the process in its entirety. The reason it's okay is because how can you truly appreciate joy without experiencing its opposite—the absence of joy?

I've also come to know that making time, the same time, each day to practice meditation has been crucial for me. And yes, sometimes, my work schedule intervenes, and when it does, I either decide to wake up even earlier because I know my day is so much better after I've practiced and centered myself, or I find a time after my first meetings to practice meditation as quickly as I can. I've also learned that skipping it one day makes it so much easier to skip it the next and then the next, and ultimately, I found myself one day completely out of practice. If I were on a baseball team or in an orchestra group and I missed significant amounts of practice, what would be the outcome of that? I wouldn't be prepared to play! Use this example in your daily life. Without practice on things that you know will center you and prepare your "lunch box" for the day, you won't be as prepared for the curve balls that everyday life can tend to throw at us from time to time.

I'd like to give you a glimpse into each day for me and where meditation fits into that so that you can take any ideas that may work and apply them to your life. In this way, the warm-up and the cooldown are just as important as the actual meditation practice, in my opinion. Much like you wouldn't just hit the court in basketball, tennis, or any other sport for that matter without taking the appropriate time to stretch and warm up and, in the end, taking time to cool down.

As soon as I wake up each morning, I stretch and immediately turn on an app on my phone called ThinkUp; this app is a positive affirmation app that allows you to choose positive affirmations that resonate with you, and then from the ones you selected, you then record those in your own voice. Now, I'm not a psychologist or any kind of doctor, so I don't know the medical facts about positive affirmations and the impact on your life. I can only speak from my experience. And, boy, let me tell you, it was a little weird at first to hear my voice coming back to me on that app each morning, but after a while, I noticed some really strong changes in how my days were starting. They started with so much more self-confidence, peace, compassion, and a true zest for life. Now, I truly know there is something so powerful about speaking positive affirmations to yourself on a regular basis, even if you aren't actively listening, and it's just running in the background.

That's how I use it. I turn on the app, and it plays for roughly twenty minutes while I'm waking up, then moving into the kitchen to make my coffee or tea. So, I can hear it, and although I'm not physically holding my phone in my hand the thoughts and affirmations are definitely sinking it. Give the ThinkUp app or a similar app a try, *I dare you*!

After my morning beverage is made, I sit down in front of my big picture window that looks out at a great big mountain in the Arizona desert and take out my mindfulness journal. This journal is only about ten pages, but I make sure to read it first thing every morning as a sort of exercise for my mind and soul. It contains in order:

1. A book *8 Verses for Training the Mind* by Kadampa Geshe Langri Tangpa. These simple yet powerful verses train my mind for the day ahead. The concept here is that for the mind to be tamed and trained is, of course, our responsibility, and the training consists of ridding ourselves of negative mental states and, instead, fostering and developing constructive ones.

2. A couple of daily prayers on compassion and gratitude that I wrote myself pertaining directly to my life and who I want to be.

3. A list of thoughtful and purposeful "*I am*" statements based on the law of resistance. The reason making a list of "*I am*" statements came to me is because I was reading a book on the universal and spiritual laws, which I will explain more in detail later. But shortly put, the law of resistance and its relation to "*I am*" statements is such a powerful tool. The law of resistance says, "What you resist will persist," and by removing *don't, can't, won't*, etc. from your words, thoughts, and beliefs and by feeling instead the joy and intention behind what you do want in your life, the universe will respond in direct proportion to who you *are*.

4. A list of statements of what *I love* based on the law of attention. I will focus more on this subject in chapter 3. But in short, this list helps me focus my attention on more of what I want for my life and then gives me strength and faith that the things I want are already on their way to my life.

5. A lengthy list of "Who I choose to be today." This list took a little time to curate, but essentially, it spells out the things I choose to let into my life or not allow into my life on a daily basis. This is a great warm-up for me.

6. A list of my daily intentions. This list is based on the universal law of intention. I will explain more of this in the next chapter. Reviewing my intentions at the start of each day helps me focus on a sort of plan for how I want my day to go, so it's much easier to stay on the track I want to travel.

After these warm-up exercises, I then get up and do some sort of exercise to warm up my body; this usually consists of yoga, weight or resistance training, or simply just stretching. Then, I shower, eat my breakfast, and move into meditation. Following this routine as well as having Oprah and Deepak as my meditation guides has really awakened the power of mindfulness within me, and it has become the absolute best part of my day.

After all of this, then I start my workday. And during my workday, if I happen to face any challenges, I can always revisit my mindfulness journal or the ThinkUp app to make me grounded again.

Once my workday is over, I make sure that I transition into an activity that is creative, like exploring a new recipe or fixing something around the house and, of course, writing. Then, I go to bed, pull out my gratitude journal, and write things I'm grateful for in the day that is now winding to a close; this helps me fall asleep in a state of gratitude, and I find that I sleep so much better and more consistently.

So if you decide to incorporate meditation into your daily life, remember these three things: be kind with yourself, practice regularly, and set realistic expectations. I have learned that even a small amount of meditation several times a week can have extraordinary effects on your life. You've got nothing to lose. It costs nothing unless you decide to build a ridiculous sanctuary like I did. Try and see how it might impact your life. I love you all and wish you the best on your journey to becoming a great meditator!

2

An Intentional Legend

Begin to use the two most powerful words, *I am* to your advantage.
How about, "*I am* receiving every good thing. *I am* happy. *I
am* abundant. *I am* healthy. *I am* love. *I am* always on time. *I
am* eternal youth. *I am* filled with energy every single day."

—The Secret

SINCE LEAVING THE state of my birth, Georgia, at the age of twenty-seven, I've lived in so many wonderful places. The first new place I called home was Virginia Beach where I really dove headfirst into my dream of becoming a hairdresser. It was during this time that I made some truly incredible friends that have remained part of my life to this day. After becoming a hairdresser, I quickly figured out that I didn't want to stop there. I wanted to—*had to*, in fact—do something that involved inspiring and educating other people. This is because I've always known that I feel my absolute best when I'm learning and sharing what I've learned with other people; this is how I know I'm a teacher at the very core of my existence.

It was a salon sales consultant that turned me on to the idea of teaching other hairdressers about a particular product brand and how to use those products to make their life and work easier and more effective in their salons. So very much like many other instances in my life, I dove in headfirst. I honestly didn't recognize it then, but

I've come to know that something far greater than myself was pulling me in that direction, and I'm so glad I jumped.

Let's just say life really took off for me after this decision, and since I decided to pursue a role in education, I've had the opportunity to travel to so many places around the world. Since that start in Virginia Beach, I've had the pleasure of living in Seattle, Miami, Salt Lake City, and now have come to call Phoenix, Arizona, my home.

When I moved to Arizona in the Spring of 2014 after a very short stint in Salt Lake City, I was very excited to start a new life there. Every time I had visited Arizona in the past, I really enjoyed the climate, the terrain, and the availability of so many outdoor activities year-round. I was also excited because Arizona, like Miami, is pretty much nonstop sunshine minus the humidity in Florida, so for me, I'd finally found the perfect balance. Now, suffice it to say, I don't enjoy sitting in the direct sun for more than a few minutes at a time. And in fact, I just can't do it because I would burn to a crisp much faster than most people; however, I remember from my time living in Seattle that, although I'm not a person that can sit in the sun, I still need to see the sun on a daily basis. Seattle was, no doubt, an incredible city and place to call home. One of the best friends I've made in my life still lives there, so I get to visit as often as I like, but I do clearly remember not being an altogether happy-go-lucky person when I lived there, and I figured out it's because, for approximately nine months of the year, the sun is banished behind so much consistent cloud cover that when it does decide to reveal itself, it really hurts your eyes, and you just stare at it because it's been missing for so long. It's really hard to explain. You'd have to live there for an amount of time to truly understand it completely.

An added bonus of living in Arizona meant that I would be much closer to my friend Saskia and, by way of that relationship, would build an incredibly strong bond with her husband Cory as well. Saskia and I worked for many years together in our education leadership roles, and we always just clicked. I never had a sister growing up, and Saskia, to me, was and is the closest possible comparison to what a female sibling will always mean to my life. She's tough on me when I need it most. We've cried with each other when we both experience things in life that just don't seem fair. We definitely laugh a ton. We share an avid love for incredible food; and it's because of this that most of our time spent together involves great drinks, outstanding cuisine, and plenty of deep, heartfelt discussions. Our favorite restaurant is Steak 44 in Phoenix, and we've spent so many occasions there discussing life, challenging each other, and ultimately cementing a friendship that will remain constant for the rest of our lives.

Since moving to Arizona, one of the things she and Cory have done from the very beginning is to infuse me into their family unit completely. I've come to know, from them, that they don't trust easily, so when they do include you, it's definitely from the heart, and you just know that you've formed a bond for life. I will always be grateful for those friendships and what it continues to teach me every day.

Saskia is naturally very open, inclusive, and nurturing. She literally can't help herself; it's just who she was born to be. Cory, her husband, on the other hand, is a completely different human. Even getting him to talk sometimes can feel like scaling the tallest mountain, and you're never quite sure what might be lingering just around the bend. But when he does speak, he never disappoints. When we are together, we never miss the opportunity to throw little jabs and be incredibly sarcastic, but it's all for the purpose of connection with no harm intended whatsoever. Sometimes, without a doubt, Saskia is concerned that we might take it a little far, but that's just her protective nature. I've learned over the years and observed in Cory that his feelings run incredibly deep, and once you've made a friend in him, you've got a friend and a brother for life. He's not the friend that is ever going to text you out of the blue, and oftentimes, he won't even respond when you text him. Let's just call that his instinctual aversion to technology and digital connection because I honestly believe digital connection holds absolutely no value for him in his life. We could all learn a lot more from him in that respect. I've come to appreciate all of this in my adopted brother. He's very thoughtful with his words, and when he does speak, it's very clear his words are well-thought-out and are delivered with the clear intention to make everyone's life better.

So, for me, meeting Saskia and Cory and having them adopt me into their family filled a void that I had for such a long time growing up. And now, I know, without a doubt, that I have a family and a safe haven in both of them. Friendships like the one I experience with them are such a valuable and rewarding gift. I'm not even sure they know it, but being around them and observing how they relate to each other and how they relate to the world is one of the greatest teachers I will have in this life.

Some of my fondest memories of my time spent with them are during the end-of-year holiday season. Every year now, I look forward to this special time because I know that we will all be gathering in Saskia and Cory's home or at her parent's house. Sometimes, it's a smaller gathering, and other times, much larger on the occasion that Cory's seven brothers and sisters can attend. Whether large or small, it's a house that is full of love, great food, and incredible conversation. Saskia's parents are such compassionate people who strive to see the good in all people and things, and over the years, I've learned so much from their wise counsel.

Choosing to write about these two great family members on the topic of being an intentional legend in life was such an easy choice. For much of my life, I knew the textbook definition of the word "intention," but Saskia and Cory brought that word and its complete meaning into the forefront of my life today and modeled what it looks like to live a life based on solid and heartfelt intentions for themselves and for the world. They are, without a doubt, incredibly intentional beings.

It's, in large part, because of my relationship with them, the reason why I started investigating how I could live a life that could be more grounded in clear and purposeful intentions.

Saskia's idea of living a life with intention is very clear. She believes for herself that clear-set intentions are one of the reasons she has a limited amount of friendships in her life. In her experience, she has more time to give quality attention and can accomplish her set intentions of being a true blessing and benefit to the lives of the people she calls her friends. She's learned from her life that spreading yourself thin with quantity over quality in relationships is an equation that never really adds up. She and Cory have intentions when it comes to their finances, retirement, raising their son Hank, as well as setting clear daily intentions for their individual growth and development. She admits the struggle is real sometimes because she has to find the balance between her intentions and still be flexible enough to experience the beauty in each and every present moment, no matter how challenging some of those moments may be.

One of the most powerful pieces of literature I've read so far on the power of your intentions and subsequently focusing your attention, which I will talk about in the next chapter, is a book called *A Little Light on the Spiritual Laws* by Diana Cooper. Her writings have become a source of comfort for me in many ways, especially on the topic and techniques available for setting your intentions and then harnessing your attention and how that can change your life. From her writings, and a few other sources, this is what I've learned about these amazing and exact spiritual laws of the universe.

A spiritual law is in a lot of ways like one of the laws of nature; for example, the law of gravity. You don't have to agree with them for them to exist. If you don't agree with the law of gravity, it doesn't mean that you're going to wake up tomorrow with the ability to fly. Spiritual laws, like natural laws, are exact. They don't have bad days. They aren't wishy-washy. They simply respond in direct proportion to the energy you give them.

The laws of intention and attention are the perfect power couple for me; they most certainly go hand in hand. Intention, simply put, means the aim and plan you hold for your life. Living a life with clear-set intentions means that you become the leading force of your experience here. You get to determine the trajectory you wish your life to take. This doesn't mean you try to control everything because I'm sure we can all agree that trying to control things and other people just doesn't work. You just do you, focus on your intentions and let your life unfold before you.

Clear-set intentions are much more than wishes, wants, and hopes; they are more strongly "what you have made up your mind to do." Visualize each intention you set for your life as an arrow in flight. When you pull back the arrow in the strings of the bow and hold it "in tension" then aim at your target, nothing can deflect it. It doesn't matter what your aim is in life. If you set it in your sights, focus your intention, and then go forward, you have set a powerful energy in motion, and the entire might of the universe will be behind your vision. So, in my case, I realized that if I wanted to write something, I could very well be taken off course, but if I set clear intentions to become a writer, then I would do anything and everything in my power to stay the course and become a writer.

Knowing that this universal law is working with you is also a good reminder to be very careful what you set your intentions to be. Positive intentions have a much higher energy, but negative intentions can still have a significant impact on others and, most especially, on your future experience of life. So please set your intentions, pull the arrow back, but my advice is to be very careful where you aim.

One of the best ways I stay on track with my intentions and where I'm aiming is the daily reviewing of my "who I choose to be today" and "my daily intentions" lists. I review these lists every morning during my morning routine, and I would like to share them with you. You can borrow any of mine or use them as a template to create your own, more personal list.

Who I Choose to Be Today

Today, I choose to guard my thoughts.
Today, I choose to guard my actions and intentions.
Today, I choose to be healthy.
Today, I choose to be considerate.
Today, I choose to grow.
Today, I choose life.
Today, I choose to be forgiving.
Today, I choose to be friendly.
Today, I choose to be grateful.
Today, I choose to show compassion.
Today, I choose to smile.
Today, I choose to be a positive example.
Today, I choose to love.
Today, I choose to enjoy all the demands of the day.
Today, I choose to appreciate the beauty of creation.
Today, I choose to help others.
Today, I choose to be conscious in thoughts, words, and actions.
Today, I choose to feel worthy.
Today, I choose to say yes to life.
Today, I choose to be open to all possibilities from the universe.
Today, I choose to love myself and others.
Today, I choose to choose my words.

My Daily Intentions

My intention is to have reverence for everyone and everything including myself, close relationships, acquaintances, people I feel distant from, people I meet in passing, people who have caused me pain, and all living things.

My intention is to write books that will help people remember who they truly are.

My intention is to be quick to forgive, slow to anger, and unbounded in love and compassion.

My intention is to eliminate from my life all gossip, judgment, sarcasm, bad habits, negative thoughts, hate, anger, fear, as well as all influences, things, and people who don't reflect my highest ideas about who I am and who I want to be.

My intention is to have a positive outlook and be grateful for all things that come into and go out of my life.

My intention is to be completely open to whatever comes into my life and whatever leaves my life without judgment, fear, or the need to control any of it.

My intention is to live today being present, not ashamed or regretful of the past, and not projecting into the future.

My intention is to attract the financial, physical, and emotional capacities to help millions of people around the world.

Make the decision today to incorporate lists like these into your routine and remember these three things to help you along your way: choose your target, aim carefully, then let go.

I have to be honest. At first, this was a frustrating task. I couldn't seem to silence the noise in my mind. Actually, I wasn't even sure what a good intention was. I knew what I wanted for my life, but I couldn't seem to put it down on paper, so when I felt lost or off course, I went to my go-to outlet. I researched anything and everything I could find on setting intentions and what that development should look like. I'm the kind of person that will usually try anything that I stumble upon if it makes a relative amount of sense. Luckily, for me, the tips were many, but at the core of them, they were all saying the same thing to me.

I wanted to summarize what I've learned from my research on setting intentions and, making sure they are in alignment with what I truly want. I've given my take on everything I've learned and put into practice with three *intention tips*:

Intention Tip 1

Be patient when envisioning your intentions. I've taken my time curating my intentions. I would encourage you to do the same. Really and truly think it over. Write it down and then edit the list. Edit it again and again until you arrive at a place where you have a clear roadmap for the direction of your life. Share it with people that you love and trust and get their insight if that will help. You could even make this a dynamic activity to share with your friends and family. You never know which member of your inner circle could benefit from this as well.

Intention Tip 2

Be extremely clear. Don't write down the first thing you think. When you think of an intention, make sure it makes you feel good, but more importantly, in keeping that intention, it will benefit other people as well. For example, if I said, "I want to become rich and successful," my intention would have a very low vibration. However, if I said, "My intention is to attract great abundance to my life so that I can share that abundance with others," the power behind an intention like that is far higher and, therefore, much more in alignment with you and the betterment of humanity as a whole. The most powerful intentions are those that benefit you and the rest of the world equally. Keep that in mind when developing the intentions for your life.

Intention Tip 3

Focus but don't try to control the outcome. This was a tough one for me in the beginning. For the longest time, I've been a bit of a control freak with all areas of my life. It wasn't until I learned how to let go of that control that I truly started living. Take my advice here: set your intentions. Make sure they are clear and in alignment with what you want your best life to be, but don't try to control the outcome every step of the way. Don't overanalyze the process either. I heard very wise words once while scrolling social media that has served as a great reminder when I feel like I want to control the outcome of the intentions I've set. I can't remember who said it, but it was so beautiful. The wise words said that setting intentions is like planting a new seed in the ground; you plant the seed (your intention), then you water it and take care of it regularly (making plans and taking action where necessary), but you don't dig the seed up every five minutes to make sure it is doing okay. If you did that, it would never grow. Let that be a reminder for all of our intentions. Plant them. Take steps that are necessary to achieve them, but don't overanalyze the rate at which your life is moving forward in the process. The flower needs time to grow. Do what you can and let the rest go!

I'm so grateful to have such close friends like Saskia and Cory, and I will continue to seek them out for guidance and to learn from them both as I move forward setting future intentions for my life. I highly recommend finding those special friends in your life and making intention setting into a fun, group activity so that you all move forward on the trajectory you wish your life to travel. It's never a bad idea to have accountability buddies close by when moving forward with your new intentions. Good friends will help keep you motivated and on track toward achieving the life you really want. The bonus is that you can do the same for them.

I truly believe that the more we grow together and share ideas, the more this world will ease out of its collective dysfunction, and we will all thrive. Wouldn't that be an amazing thing for everyone?

3

An Attentive Legend

The day you decide that you are more interested in being
aware of your thoughts than you are in the thoughts
themselves—that is the day you will find your way out.

—Michael Singer

I FIND IT quite easy to adapt to most locations around the world. Most of my professional career led to constant jet setting around the globe and kept me in a state of perpetual jetlag, so I naturally became accustomed to it. I also enjoy many climates around the world. I love experiencing different cultures and customs and take every opportunity to learn something new when I'm traveling. It's in the moments where I've traveled to different countries that I learn the most, simply by observing how other people live and interact with one another. These moments have taught me so much about how we are all truly connected as human beings no matter how many miles separate us.

However, all bets are off when it comes to the cold weather. I've always been that way. Me not doing well in cold weather is quite the understatement. In my mind, I love the ideas that are conjured from pictures of snow-covered mountains, ski resorts, and sitting by a nice roaring fire because it all creates this sense of peace for me. All of these things would be great if I could enjoy them without ever having to actually step foot outside once the temperature falls below 60 degrees Fahrenheit.

It's because of this aversion to cold weather that I don't get to spend as much time as I truly would like to with my dear friend Amy. She is raising a family and running a very successful salon, which keeps her incredibly busy throughout the year. She does manage to make a trip to Arizona every couple of years, and I'm extremely grateful for those times. I wish I could visit her more often, but again, it's not possible because in Edmonton, Alberta, where she lives, it's only above 60 degrees Fahrenheit for about six weeks every year. I have visited her twice in Edmonton, during the middle of the winter for work-related events, and she can attest to my serious debilitation when confronted with cold weather.

I'm sure most of you have heard the expression "Brother from another mother" when referring to a friend that is as close to you if not closer than the family you were born into. To give a twist on that expression, Amy is, without a doubt, my "sister from another mister." Truly, deep connections in life I don't think always come with an explanation and, quite honestly, any attempt at defining them would only scratch the surface of the life-sustaining ability those connections truly embody. Amy is that friend and confidant for me and has been from the moment we first met.

Like a few other special people that have become a part of my daily life, Amy and I also met through work in 2009. We were both education leaders for the same hair care brand, which meant we were guaranteed quality hang time two to three times per year. We manage, no matter what, to connect over the phone or video chat once or twice a month just to catch up, laugh about current experiences, and yes, sometimes cry through the pain and aggravation of life-altering events. Being able to laugh with a friend is a true gift for sure, but for me, being able to cry with one permanently ties your souls to each other, and you just know that you've got a friend for life. It's a true pleasure to call Amy one of my soulmates, and I look ahead to many more years of laughter, tears, and incredible growth in life. I hope that everyone has a friend or can find a friend like Amy because I know your life will be so much more enriched because of that connection.

One of my favorite times spent with Amy was in Minneapolis in 2015 during the summer months, no doubt. Suffice it to say, I don't think you will find me in Minnesota during any months except June, July, and August.

We were there together for a company-related educator training, and because we were both in education leadership roles, the opportunities for quiet and private connection were definitely limited. Nevertheless, one of the evenings before our group dinner we did manage to sneak away with a glass of wine under some lovely shade trees outside of the hotel, just out of eyeshot of anyone that might come outside. I remember we sat at a little wrought iron table enjoying our beverage and picked up our conversation as if no time had passed. We laughed a lot, although quietly, so that we wouldn't be discovered.

I remember during this time I was having a particular challenge processing some old trauma in regard to my family dynamic and specifically the relationship with my brother. It was no surprise, like always in my experience with Amy, that her response and the advice that she shared were well considered and perfectly delivered. I recall her saying something along the lines of, "Maybe you're just giving it too much attention. Maybe, my friend, it's time to truly let that go." She nor I could have imagined the impact that advice would go on to have in my life, but I'm so thankful for that special moment with my soulmate Amy; the person who can often see me better than I can see myself.

Amy really helped me navigate and understand that crucial yet failed relationship with my brother and the source of pain it would continue to be if I didn't find a way to resolve it. I will always be grateful to her for the words of encouragement and wisdom during this time where I was aching for solace and struggling to find a way to forgive him for the impact he had on my life.

My brother was held captive to drug addiction for many years growing up. His struggle with drug abuse caused quite a lot of collateral damage to me and our family. I remember being frustrated on many occasions when I would, for example, be receiving an academic award in school, I would look out in the audience and would notice that my mother wasn't there because she was, no doubt, dealing with some trouble he had gotten himself into. He also spent quite a lot of time in prison during my young adult years, and I remember being so angry with him because, in my mind, drugs were something you could just say yes or no to, and he was clearly choosing to say yes to those drugs and say no to being a big brother and role model for me. Of course, I've never been addicted to them, so my understanding of the incapacitating effect and total control they can have over you was very limited. In more recent years, I've done a substantial amount of reading on the topic and have become much more educated on the struggles of living a life captivated by neurological altering substances.

I carried this grief, frustration, and anger about my brother with me for so many years until, after a great amount of reading, soul searching, and asking myself deeply personal and exploratory questions, I was able to see my way out of the confusion and start to heal the deep emotional scars that were caused by this experience. Healing those scars has been one of the most pivotal moments in my life that has allowed me to start paying much more attention to what I'm paying attention to. With my brother, it's allowed me to move into a healing space where I can see his drug addiction as a gift. I know that may sound strange to many of you reading this, but I have chosen to believe that by witnessing him doing drugs, being addicted to drugs, and all the trouble that came along because of them, I never chose to use drugs. In a way, he kept me safe and kept me from having to endure those horrible experiences because he showed me firsthand why I shouldn't choose that path. It's taken me many years, but now, I am simply grateful to my brother for protecting me, even though that wasn't his intention. Being able to find the true gift in such a tragic experience has allowed me to move into a space of my life where I look for the gift and the lesson in so many more experiences, especially those that are challenging. I've come to know that many things can be solved simply by changing the focus of your attention in your life.

Remember from the previous chapter where I talked about universal laws. The universal law of attention states that if you give 20 percent of your attention to something, the universe will respond with a 20 percent outcome. The universe isn't judgmental in any way; it simply responds exactly to your request.

Think about it this way; if you are taking a road trip somewhere, this can be one of the best illustrations of the law of attention at work. What would happen if you weren't giving your attention to the road signs, speed limits, and the other cars on the road. You could end up in an accident, get a speeding ticket, and if you're anything like me, you could end up at the wrong destination. Trust me, yes, this has happened on more occasions than I would like to admit.

Imagine the last time you experienced some level of physical pain in your body. When you gave all of your attention to the pain, did it hurt more or less? Remember the last time you missed someone, and you focused the majority of your attention on missing them. Did you end up missing them more or less? Here is the last example and my absolute favorite; recall the last time you were genuinely missing a friend and really wanted to talk to them, and so you put a lot of your attention on how fun that conversation would be. Can you remember how you felt when, out the blue, they called you to say they were thinking about you?

Simply put, the law of attention responds to your words, actions, and thoughts with extreme precision. Knowing this, I caution you, friends, to pay close attention to what you are paying attention to.

Now, fast forward to our collective human experience today. I'm sure you've all noticed that most stories on the news, most posts on social media, most conversations you may overhear, and probably, the conversations you're actually involved in are about one thing: *fear*. Fear in uncertainty, fear in losing something or someone, fear in other people, fear in becoming overweight, fear in becoming too thin, fear in not having enough followers, fear in not making enough money, fear in having less than others, and fear in not looking like a supermodel; the examples are endless.

When I do manage to turn on the news, which isn't often anymore, or scroll through social media, which is even less often, I'm not surprised, but I am truly saddened at the amount of content that is constantly being presented to us twenty-four hours a day with one true goal at its core: to make us afraid, worried, unsure, angry, self-doubting, lacking, and never quite good enough. How did this happen? When did we stop spreading positivity?

Now, I'm not saying the people who report the news are bad people. They are doing a job they are being paid to do, but I do think it's worth mentioning that because of television ratings and how that system works, they only continue to report what we collectively respond to. It's the same idea behind supply and demand in a grocery store. If we collectively stopped buying tons of junk food and chose more healthy options, the grocery store chains and the food industry would swiftly make those healthy options more readily available and at a better price, no doubt. The same goes for the media. If we stopped paying attention to the negative news, they would have no choice but to eventually change what they are reporting.

No matter what, the same laws of the universe apply to these strange and challenging times we are all experiencing. Remember, the law of attention is *exact*. So if we give our attention to worry, fear, self-doubt, and not having enough, guess what, we are collectively energizing those emotions. It's that kind of collective attention that has allowed those emotions to run rampant for decades now.

There is light at the end of the tunnel though. You can still choose what you want to see in your life. I think Deepak Chopra said it very well in one of his guided meditations when he said, "The situation out there, reflects the situation in here." Very powerful words in my opinion. My research on the universal law of attention has also taught me that positive attention has a much more powerful energy than negative attention so you can use this to your advantage in life. Shift your attention to more positive things and watch your life and your experience of life become much more positive. I guess the best way for me to articulate everything I have learned on this subject is just to say; if you don't want something or someone in your life, then don't give it or them any attention whatsoever. It truly works!

If you want that dream job, give it your positive attention. If you want that special someone to come into your life, give it your positive attention. If you want your business to become more profitable, give it your positive attention.

From experience, I feel compelled to share with you that shifting your attention is not going to be a cakewalk; it will take dedication, practice, and perseverance. I read something that Oprah

Winfrey said not long ago that really helped me hone the power of my attention. She said, "One of the hardest things in life to learn is which bridges to cross and which bridges to burn." This resonated with me on such a deep and personal level, and it allowed me to start seeing the things I was paying attention to as bridges to the future life that I truly want. The question for all of us is: Which things in my life are bridges I'm going to choose to keep, and which things in my life are bridges that I may need to burn?

With my brother, his drug abuse and the trauma that I carried for many years surrounding that relationship, I've grown to understand that I no longer have to pay attention to the negative impact. I can choose to move forward, giving it the positive attention of being one of the greatest gifts I've ever received; a gift that has, no doubt, shaped my adult life for the better.

One of the best ways I practice being an attentive legend is by using "*I love*" statements. During my morning alone time, I review my list of "*I love*" statements as a reminder of what I would like to focus my attention on for the day in order to attract more of those things to my life, and then I just have faith that those things are on their way to me. It's important to point out that I've made sure each statement of the things I love will benefit others as much as it would benefit my life. I recite each statement ten times to myself silently; again, just as a way to ground my day and set me on the path I want to travel. Here are those statements below. Please feel free to use them and make some of your own.

I Love Statements

I love me and other people!
I love being a creator with the universe!
I love being a better person!
I love wealth and abundance to share more with others!
I love winning and helping others win!
I love knowing how things work!
I love knowing why things work!
I love being positive!
I love being compassionate!
I love learning new things to teach new things!
I love being healthy!
I love helping others!
I love consciousness!
I love writing things that help me and help others!
I love harnessing the power of my attention!

Let's face it and face it together! Fact is, you may not like how things are going right now in your life, and that's okay. We've all been there and will be there again at some point in life. You may not agree with people that "seem" to have power over your happiness, but here is one of the greatest secrets of life. You have way more influence than you realize, and you hold that influence in the power of your attention. In fact, Mahatma Gandhi referred to the influence that you have as "truth force, love force, soul force." It is definitely a power that you own that allows you to conjure the very best in people. It is a power that you own that allows you to change people's hearts and minds just by the way you choose to see them; by changing the way you observe them. That's really all it takes. It's that easy.

Nobel physicist Max Plank said it best when he said, "When you change the way you look at things, the things you look at change." Isn't that just so profound? Does it resonate with you? In fact, scientists have been able to prove, for example, that if a college professor is told that one particular student in their class has a higher IQ, that student's IQ automatically rises to meet the professor's expectations, and they've never even met or had a conversation. So you see, simply expecting the best in people brings out the best in people; this is universal law. Remember, it's extremely *exact*; therefore, the opposite of that statement is also true—expecting the worst in people will no doubt bring out the worst in them. The power of your consciousness is absolute. You have the ability inside of you to conjure the very best or the absolute worst in people solely based on how you choose to see them. We all have the power to change every heart and mind on the planet, simply by changing our own hearts and minds; this is how consciousness begins to spread like a virus. And that, my friends, is the kind of virus that this planet and humanity very much needs.

Here's the bitter pill to swallow sometimes; we all have darkness in us, but don't let that scare you. It just is what it is. Darkness in all of us is inevitable, and simply disagreeing with it doesn't make the darkness cease to exist. Just accept that darkness is in all of us, but that also means we all have a light inside of us too. And in every moment of our life, we are given the choice of letting darkness rule or allowing the light to reign over our consciousness. Just because the darkness exists, it doesn't mean you have to access it for any reason whatsoever. You can leave it there untouched for your entire life; it's your choice. What you stand as a witness for in others will automatically strengthen or weaken in the other person because we are all truly interconnected. So when you look at the worst in someone, when you make them wrong in your mind and refuse to see the best in them, you are committing a spiritual assault of the worst kind against them because, in that moment, you are essentially testifying that they have no ability to choose the light; you are standing witness for the darkness in them which will, you guessed it, call forth more darkness in them and in you.

Look at it this way, we have all, most likely, experienced the hostile force of a stranger, a loved one, a police officer, a partner, or maybe, even witnessed the hostility of a crowd on television. We've all felt another person's contempt for us at one point or another in our lives. You've, no doubt, felt the incredibly destructive force and power of that contempt in the moment of hostility, and you've felt its residual effect for long after the encounter. But here's the reality, you still have a choice. You can choose not to give in to this mindset; this way of seeing things (darkness) in others. Simply stand and affirm the light in other people, especially in moments of hostility, and just see what happens. Whether we are always able to see it or not, there is an unassailable spark of divine light in every living thing on this planet, and it's just waiting for you to call it forward.

When you call on that divine light in someone else, you are giving it permission to reign in their lives and bring peace, love, and compassion forth in them. The power of your divine witness for other people calls forth the divine truth in them. It calls for the love in their hearts, the grace, and beauty in their soul; that's why I believe that divine witnessing of this magnitude is the most powerful form of nonviolence that we should all be embracing. It heals the very root of violence. It turns your enemies into friends, even when you thought they were deplorable and wrong. In any situation where you see no light, dig deep and make your own light. Call upon that divine essence within you to reveal itself in you and shape your reality. Now, can you imagine if more and more people start to do this? What would our planet and humanity look like moving forward?

So now, to all of you, the truth in me calls out to the truth in you. Look for the best in all people and all circumstances, especially when it feels difficult. It's the only thing I want to continue to see in others because I have experienced its power and its ability to completely restructure my life and the way I see the lives of others. Learning this power and truth of the universe more each day is what allows me to see everyone, and I do mean everyone as my friend. For me, to condemn you is the same thing as condemning myself because we are all the same energy. We all come from the same star stuff, so I choose to regard you as true, good, wise, and kind. And so, it will be because that is what we all want to see, deep down, in parts of our soul that we haven't even experienced yet.

Pay *attention*, dear friends, much more often to the things you want in your life and how you would like to see your life change because what you pay attention to will, without a doubt, expand and shape your reality. You get to decide every day. So the only question that should remain is: What do you want your reality to be?

A Satisfied Legend

A satisfied life is better than a successful life. Because
our success is measured by others, but our satisfaction
is measured by our own soul, mind, and heart.

—Unknown

THE YEAR 2020, without a doubt, presented all of us with a litany of
challenges, emotions, and suffering. At the end of 2019, we started
to hear whispers of a novel and highly infectious virus, originating in
China, that could potentially have a pandemic impact on everyone
around the world. A virus had not altered the course of human history in such an enormous way since the Spanish influenza of 1918.

I remember being at a beautiful resort in Mexico, during the
first part of 2020, for a sales conference when COVID-19 became a
very real thing. This sales conference was the biggest event we held
each year, and when they announced that we would be canceling
the event and all associated activities, I made the quick decision to
change my flight and return home the next morning. I wasn't sure
what would happen in relation to border closures and didn't want the
chance of being stuck in a foreign country while the virus continued
to spread.

Across the world, we may have all been in the same storm, but
we were also in our own individual ships through this experience.

As the virus continued to spread rapidly, governments had to make decisions on which businesses to temporarily close and which ones to allow to remain open. For the small businesses, these forced closures, although temporary, had an immediate impact and would, no doubt, prove to have a detrimental effect for years to come. Unemployment rates skyrocketed around the world. Many people lost their homes, their jobs, and their loved ones who succumbed to the virus; these were excruciatingly painful times for everyone for so many different reasons. Life, as we knew it, no longer existed.

As much as I wanted to keep up to date on the battle of this new virus, I had to make the decision to read the news rather than watch it because watching it only brought on more fear and anxiety. This was the story of the decade—if not, the century—and it's all anyone and everyone could talk about. I chose to play it safe, keep my distance, and only venture out when absolutely necessary. I didn't want to be a secret carrier of the virus and unknowingly pass it on to someone who might not survive it.

So, from March of that year, I was officially on lockdown at my home in Arizona. I was used to traveling around the world on a weekly basis, and now, I was on lockdown; this was new territory for me, to say the least. What was I going to do? I've always enjoyed my alone time; time to rest and recharge, but this period of isolation proved to be challenging, heartbreaking, and presented me with a plethora of other emotions that, at the time, I wasn't prepared for, but now, looking back, I'm so grateful for the experience of living in isolation for the better part of a year.

Very early on, I stumbled across a movie called *Life Itself* directed by Dan Fogelman released in 2018. This movie changed my life and the way I viewed my current experience, to say the least. *Life Itself* centers on a couple played by Oscar Isaac and Olivia Wilde that lead a multigenerational love story spanning both decades and continents, from the streets of New York to the Spanish countryside, and are all connected by a single event. College sweethearts Will and Abby fall in love, get married, and prepare to bring their first child into the world. As their story unfolds in New York, fate links them to a group of people in Seville, Spain, including a troubled young woman, a man and his granddaughter, a wealthy landowner, and a plantation manager.

I highly recommend everyone to watch this movie. It provoked so many emotions in me and had a huge impact on the way I choose to view my daily life and everything we experience during life as a whole. Without a doubt, the most profound moment in the movie for me is toward the end when the narrator says, "Life will bring you to your knees," but she goes on to explain that it doesn't do so to cause us pain. It does so to give you the gift of humility. Almost immediately, I made the conscious choice to start viewing what was happening all around the world as a gift of humility and, as with any gift, what I could be taking away from this new adaptation to life that would bring me peace and help me grow.

My new level of growth started with a simple yet complex question. I had no doubt achieved a great amount of success in my life, but was I *satisfied*?

I had now been given all of this alone time. What was I going to do with it? I had to choose between letting it drive me crazy or getting busy, and getting busy is exactly what I did. I started with my house. I ordered a large dumpster to be delivered, and I went through the process of gutting the inside of my house to the studs in most rooms. I pulled up the carpet and tile. I tore down the drywall. I combined electrical switches, so they made more sense to me. The house, since I purchased it, had always felt sort of closed in, so I went the opposite direction and opened it up as much as I could. During this time, I simply turned the music up and let inspiration and instinct be my guide for the new home I wanted to create from the inside out. I should point out that I have no former training in this kind of project, but thanks to YouTube and some additional sources, I took projects on slowly and called in reinforcements only when necessary.

During this experience, I started contemplating the connection that this rigorous and physical altering of my home could have to other areas of my life. In essence, I started having long-overdue conversations with myself on how good it felt to be breathing new life into my house and how that same approach could be applied to creating more satisfaction in all other areas of my life. The physical pain and exhaustion I experienced ripping up porcelain tiles and tearing down walls didn't even come close to comparing with the pain and exhaustion I would end up experiencing in parts of my life that included toxic relationships; unhappiness at work; and my overall physical, mental, and emotional wellbeing. Much like the renovation of my home, it was time to start editing my life ruthlessly and let instinct and inspiration be my guide.

The two areas we spend most of our time are with other people and in our jobs. I started with my relationships, all relationships, and this is what I learned.

Relationship Renovation Project 1

The direction of your life is your responsibility! Any relationship you're currently engaged in that isn't leading you in the direction that you genuinely want your life to go, you have to address it, correct any behaviors possible, or simply move away from the relationship; this isn't easy. It involves a lot of courage and wisdom to speak up, know the right words to use in conversation, and simply walk away from it if that's the best solution.

Relationship Renovation Project 2

Avoid abuse at all costs! If the relationship demonstrates any form of abuse (emotional, verbal, and physical), then you must make the determined decision to choose yourself first, make your needs the top priority, and set firm boundaries. Abuse in any form doesn't have to be happening to you; it could be happening in your presence. For example, someone who has any sort of alcohol or drug addiction is abusing themselves and, thereby, abusing your position in their life. They are counting on you to be there for them while they hurt themselves; this creates a stronghold of codependency. Trust me, you will not fix another person no matter how hard you try. They are the only person that can want to fix themselves; that's just one example. Another is having a "friend" that is constantly putting other people down. They are demonstrating abuse for others, so what makes you think they aren't speaking similarly about you when your back is turned? Walk away from any form of abuse as quickly and safely as you possibly can.

Relationship Renovation Project 3

Are you the perpetrator? Be the change you want to see. Let's face it; sometimes, in a toxic relationship, you are the perpetrator. We are human beings and, therefore, not perfect. If you discover that you are the one inflicting pain on the relationship, then take the necessary steps to permanently correct your behavior. Ask for their forgiveness and then be willing to accept the consequences of your actions in the relationship. If they choose that it is best for them to move on without you in their life, don't hold it against them. Grant them the grace and compassion for making the best choice for their life.

Relationship Renovation Project 4

Don't beg for a relationship! If someone truly wants to be in your life, they will make the effort to do so. If people are showing you through their actions that they don't want to be in your life completely, then believe them. Don't chase people. Don't beg people to be your friend or your partner in life. If you are the one constantly making the effort to connect, then the relationship is definitely out of balance, one-sided, and will lead you to a lot of unnecessary emotional pain. Stand firm in the knowledge that you are a beautiful person and are absolutely deserving, and the people that are meant to be in your life will be there. Instead of focusing your energy on the ones that constantly disappoint you, give your time and energy to the people that truly show up in your life.

Relationship Renovation Project 5

Relatives don't always mean family! This one has been the most difficult for me. The group of people that you are born into are your *relatives*; that doesn't always mean that those people are your *family*. I've come to believe through experience that you get to choose your family as you grow. Don't fall victim to the guilt and anguish that your relatives can inflict on you. They are just people as well, making the best choices they can for their life. The choices they make and have made are based on their life experience; don't hold it against them. You can be cordial with your relatives, but being related to someone doesn't mean that you have to continue a relationship with them; it's still your choice. Do what's best for you, and surround yourself with the people that make you happy, make you feel appreciated, and support you in the good and bad times without judgment.

Now, for the area where we spend another large amount of time: our jobs. For most of us, having a job is essential. We need to work to pay the bills and enhance our quality of life for ourselves and our families. On average, each of us spends approximately one-third of our time each year at work. So my question to you is: Are you enjoying what you do for work?

In October of 2020, after being with the same organization for thirteen years, I made the decision to leave that job and pursue a more positive, encouraging, and nurturing work environment. Don't get me wrong, I loved my job, the time spent there, and the wonderful relationships I cultivated throughout the years. Still, thanks to all of my newfound time in solitude, I was able to examine the course of my professional life and make the decision to edit that part ruthlessly as well.

As much as I loved being a part of the team and thoroughly enjoyed all of the projects that I was able to participate in, I felt something even stronger in my gut. I was existing in a role where I felt the two worst things that I could imagine in a job: taken for granted and taken advantage of. So I made the decision to part ways and take on an exciting role with a new company that would cele-brate my skillset and that would allow me creative freedom to utilize those skills in constructing something amazing. Here is what I have come to know from that experience.

Job Renovation Project 1

If it doesn't make you happy, don't do it! Yes, for most of us, a job is an essential task during our lives. Given that you spend a third of your time working, please make it something you truly enjoy doing. Aligning your job with your true purpose and passion in life is critical. I'm not saying to go out and quit your job tomorrow; you can be smart about it. Put money aside that would make parting ways a lot more comfortable and, during that time of saving, start drafting your ideas of what your perfect job would look like. Then, start searching for how to make that job come into your life. You will be so happy you did.

Job Renovation Project 2

Don't be taken for granted! If you're a go-getter like I am, celebrate that characteristic; however, don't let yourself exist in a professional position where your efforts are overlooked and taken for granted. Speak up for what you believe you deserve. In the end, if you don't get what you feel you deserve, at least you have your answer. You can stand proud in the knowledge that you stood up for yourself, and you can start searching for an environment that makes you truly happy and appreciated.

Job Renovation Project 3

Don't be taken advantage of! When you're a hard worker, it's normal practice in most organizations for your plate to become full and, oftentimes, overflowing with responsibility. Companies often-times give more and more responsibility to the employees that prove themselves time and time again. Unfortunately, what those companies don't measure is how much additional responsibility can stretch your limits and ultimately burn you out. Speak up for the tasks you can realistically handle and then find the kindest way to communicate that you can't take on any more without additional help and support. Being a "yes" person all the time doesn't work out, trust me. It's your respon-sibility to put items on your plate that you can realistically accomplish. This ensures that you give your best to the tasks at hand, and you don't end up in a situation where you are spreading yourself too thin in your work and, therefore, not giving each project your best effort.

The time and energy we spend with others in relationship and the time we spend at work for the longest time have been the measur-ing template for what we see as our success in life. I want to encour-age you to think about it differently. Since you spend the majority of your life in relationship to others at work or in your personal lives, those two places should be the measuring template for how satis-fied you are in life. Success is an illusion, satisfaction is a guaranteed life-affirming quality. What can we do to eliminate the illusion of success and start living a more satisfying life experience?

Success is insatiable; it's a thirst that can't be quenched. It's driven and measured by external motivators and external validation. It is not the key to happiness. On the contrary, happiness (satisfaction) is the key to success. History has taught us that measuring your life based on a higher salary, more superiority, more notoriety, more acclaim, and more visibility is essentially putting the cart before the horse, so to speak, in relation to living a satisfying life. Look at some of the most famous entertainers in modern history: Whitney Houston, Prince, and Michael Jackson to name a few. All indications of their success practically scream that they were not happy. Successful, in the eyes of the public, absolutely; satisfied in their own private lives and thoughts, absolutely not. Knowing that, I strongly encourage you to pursue satisfaction in your life, not success. Here are some great ways to get started.

Keep a gratitude journal

Finding time daily to jot down all of the things you are grateful for is a great way to center your thinking and draw attention to how many great things and people you have in your life. Pick a time every day or week to sit down and write about your good fortune. Let your mind reflect on what went right or what you are grateful for. Sometimes, it helps to pick a number—such as three to five things—that you will identify each day or week. As you write, be as specific as you can and be mindful to feel the sensations you felt when something good happened to you.

Embrace altruism

Altruism is the complete opposite of selfishness. It involves doing things for others with absolutely no expectation of reward. The kind act of helping others feels good and brings so many rewards to your life. It reduces the feeling of isolation and creates a sense of belonging. It helps you keep things that are happening in your life in perspective, especially when your altruism is directed at someone less fortunate. It's no doubt contagious and helps the world become a much happier place. The biggest benefit in my opinion is that the more you help others, the more you are actually helping yourself. Embracing altruism is one of the sure-fire ways to a more satisfying life.

Take responsibility for your joy

Your joy is your responsibility; it's only *your* responsibility. When you operate from the mindset that nobody can make you happy, then it stands true that nobody can make you sad. My favorite way to ensure joy in my life is to check in on how I'm feeling regularly and also never forgetting to check that my boundaries for my life are in place and being reaffirmed on a regular basis. When you take the wheel as the only driver of your happiness, you start changing your past conditioning and start to see more and more things to be satisfied with in your life.

Personally, I've stopped focusing on success completely; rather, I've decided to run full steam ahead into cultivating a more satisfying life. I've come to understand that as long as I'm doing what I truly enjoy and surrounding myself with the people who are moving in the same direction toward satisfaction, then my life is beyond successful; it is a life that is complete.

An Attractive Legend

> Maybe the journey isn't so much about *becoming* anything.
> Maybe it's about *unbecoming* everything that isn't really you,
> so you can be who you were meant to be in the first place.

—Paul Coelho

I NEVER REALLY got into video games growing up. I'm from the age of Atari and computer games on a Commodore 64. So by the time Nintendo and Sega hit the scene, I'd decided I wasn't interested. Don't get me wrong, getting lost in hours of playing Pitfall and Donkey Kong were great for what they were, but I moved on quickly and found other things to do. My brother stuck with video games for the majority of his teenage and young adult years. I guess to each his own and that's okay by me.

As I approach my mid-forties, and after experiencing many of the things that I have in life, I honestly wish I would have spent a little more time with video games, especially concentrating on the parts where you learn how to move from one level to the next with much more ease.

Have you ever felt like you have been stuck on the same level in life and keep experiencing the same situations and people over and over? I've definitely felt like that before. And in those times, I remember getting incredibly frustrated, wondering how many times

I would have to experience the same hurtful or disappointing thing. With a video game, it's rather easy. You pay attention to the obstacles that you are being presented with, and when you fail to pass a certain level, you know that you can go back and try again, and the obstacles will be exactly the same, so you are prepared.

With life, it's not that cut and dry. The challenge may be the same, but each time you experience it again, the landscape has changed; you have changed. With that said, it's understandable that it's not going to be as easy as remembering the obstacles from the previous experience and just looking out for those. The obstacles have changed because the entire landscape has changed.

We are constantly evolving humans. In my case, I finally learned that I would keep repeating those experiences until I actually learned the lesson and made the conscious choice to level up no matter how the landscape looked at the time. I've also come to truly know that whatever I'm experiencing in life is a true reflection of what and who I am on the inside. As mentioned before, Deepak Chopra clearly says, "The situation out there reflects the situation in here." In a nutshell, you and *only you* are attracting everything and every person that you experience into your life.

I met one of my greatest and lifelong friends Luis during a trip to Las Vegas in 2006. I had traveled to Nevada for an annual conference hosted by the beauty industry. My cousin happened to live in Las Vegas, so I was able to visit with him as well during my downtime. One evening, he invited me to a dinner party hosted by a couple of his friends. I'm a self-proclaimed wallflower at social events, so the idea of going to a dinner party and having to interact with complete strangers was not my idea of a great evening, but my cousin really wanted me there, so I went.

Luis must have sensed my discomfort with strange people, and he instantly welcomed me and got me introduced to the other people at the party. I don't know how to explain it, but we became instant friends. When I lived in Seattle for a few years, it cemented our relationship more and made it unbreakable. We share so many memories of birthday celebrations, social gatherings, and dinners, and every time, him knowing that I'm not instantly comfortable with strangers, he would continue to wrap his arms around me and show me the way. We've been through breakups together and the loss of family members, and each time, our friendship flourishes. Not having the greatest big brother role model growing up, Luis has, without question, stepped into that role and given more to my life in that respect than I could have imagined. We often know exactly what the other is thinking. Even after leaving Seattle, I've made trips there just to catch up and continue the bond with my great friend. He has recently been pursuing his dream of becoming a shoe and wardrobe designer, and it's been a pleasure to watch him achieve every dream he has set for himself.

If I'm a self-proclaimed wallflower, then Luis is a tried-and-true social butterfly. In any given room of people, it's been a known fact that he will know approximately half of them; that's just how it has always been since I've known him. He goes out of his way to make everyone feel comfortable in any given setting. It's one of the qualities that has endeared him as one of my best friends and closest confidants. I've also come to discover over the years of our friendship that he is the absolute personification of the law of attraction.

The law of attraction is a universal law. Whether you believe in it or not, it still goes on existing and shaping the lives that we live. Put simply, the law of attraction teaches us that like attracts like. We attract people and situations into our life based on the energy we have inside of us and the signals we are pushing out to the universe based on that energy. This law is not wishy-washy; it is incredibly exact. Everything and everyone that you experience is a direct reflection of how you truly feel about yourself. Look around you and notice the people and things in your life. Our underlying beliefs attract the things that we experience. For example, if you believe that you are undeserving, you will attract people into your life who absolutely mirror your belief back to you by treating you poorly.

Negative aspects like neediness, greed, depression, desperation, being unkind, and thoughtlessness all have a very low-frequency vibration and, most likely, happen unconsciously. On the contrary, qualities like compassion, gratitude, love, kindness, respect, and generosity all have a very high-frequency vibration and happen more often in the conscious, self-aware person. Negative and positive both are like magnets, and they will attract people and situations with those qualities into your life; it's the exact universal law.

The inner attracts the outer. You can argue with that, but it won't stop being true. Examine your life, and if you are happy with every aspect, then keep moving in that direction; however, if you see something or someone in your life that you do not like, change the way you feel about yourself inside and then watch how the law of attraction will shift and work alongside you and in your favor.

This universal law, although complex on many levels, is really quite simple. You attract into your life exactly what you think and believe about yourself. If you don't like your current situation, then change your belief about yourself and watch the energies shift. If you feel like you are underserving of great things, then you will continue to attract people that treat you poorly. If you feel like you *have to* support people, then you will continue to attract needy people that want you to fix them.

The law of attraction is one of the great mysteries of life. Very few of us are actually aware of how much impact the law of attraction has on our daily lives. Consciously or unconsciously, every moment in our life, we are like human magnets projecting our thoughts and emotions and attracting back to us more of what we have projected. Unfortunately, many of us are still completely unaware of the potential that is locked away within us. It is far too simple and seemingly more comfortable to let our thoughts and emotions go unchecked. Unfortunately, however, this sends out the wrong signals to the universe and attracts more of the emotions and events that you don't want in your life.

There is hope still. When you discover and fully accept that the law of attraction is working within your life, you will be able to harness it and, in turn, celebrate everything that is to come. Once you truly understand and embrace the key behind the law of attraction, you will be renewed with hope and courage in the knowledge that you are completely free to take the reins of your life, and in doing so, you will free yourself from the vicious and counterproductive cycles of fear, worry, or negativity, which have held you back for far too many years.

Some of the greatest minds and biggest success stories throughout history give direct credit to the law of attraction. Based on research, the concept of this universal law can be found in ancient Buddhist and Christian teachings. Buddha said that our thoughts make us what we are. Jesus's teachings have been interpreted to give us insight into our unique ability to create from within. In more recent history, there have been countless books and articles published on the topic, so its notoriety continues to grow as we continue to evolve. More recently, one of the greatest sports stars, Michael Jordan, said, "In order to do great things, you have to think great things first."

After the groundbreaking and awe-inspiring publications from Helena Blavatsky and Thomas Troward in the nineteenth century on the topic, many authors in more modern history have penned their own unique take on the power of this law and, in many cases, even documented its proven effectiveness through personal success stories. As with any subject, and considering the vast array of interpretations, I set out to find the most common ways to incorporate the law of attraction into my daily life, and this is what I found.

Step 1

Know what you truly want (and don't want). Knowing what you truly want and, equally as important, what you don't want in your life is much more than half the battle. Whether you are focused on making significant advances in your professional or personal development, knowing what you want to experience and what you would like to leave behind is crucial to experiencing the life you want moving forward. A tool that has always worked well for me, usually at the end of each year, is to take the time to make a list of the things I want in my life moving forward and the things that I do not. I do recommend writing this list somewhere that you can review it on a regular basis. Once you have the list in front of you, it's far easier to map out your game plan on how to move forward in your newly decided life direction. This list can change and evolve as you change and evolve. The most important thing, in my opinion, is to keep the list accessible so that you can make adjustments and track your progress. This doesn't have to be a daunting project, make it fun. Go with the flow and make adjustments to your list as necessary. Regardless of how the list evolves over time, adopt the mindset that you are exactly where you are supposed to be in the present moment. Setbacks will no doubt happen, but setbacks don't have to determine your destiny. They can and should be visualized as an essential part of your growth and development toward the life of your dreams.

Step 2

Focus on gratitude. One of the main reasons I love keeping a gratitude journal is so I can go back and review it from time to time to see how my life is progressing toward my dreams. It always gives me an extra boost of encouragement when I can see something, I wrote on my list a year ago that has now become a part of my daily life. I've learned firsthand that when you write down things you are grateful for and truly adopt an attitude of gratitude, you attract more and more things into your life for which you can be grateful.

Step 3

Practice intentional communication and positive self-talk; this one is a biggie for me. I've learned there is a vast difference between saying "*I am*" something and "*I want to be*" something. Emphatically stating that you "*are*" something has a much stronger frequency than you "*want to be*" something. Saying "*I am*" carries a lot more weight and energy than simple wishful thinking. The former vibrates at a much higher frequency, and then the universe has no choice but to respond in direct proportion to that frequency. With that said, I should stress that you will want to be very thoughtful and intentional about the things that you do and don't want. Mindfully, be very careful what you declare to the universe because it will respond in direct relationship to the amount of intention and energy you give your declarations. It's also very important to understand that positive intentions vibrate at a much higher frequency than negative ones. This goes for the words that you use as well. Life has taught us that positive affirmations are far more likely to come into your life more quickly than negative affirmations; however, negative affirmations about yourself or others have the ability to keep you stuck and prevent you from taking your life to the next level. Stop the vicious cycle of saying negative things about others, and absolutely stop the cycle of stating negative things about yourself. If you make statements like "I'm never going to accomplish this," for example, then the universe has no choice but to respond and keep you from achieving your dreams.

Step 4

Visualize satisfaction; this is, without a doubt, my favorite part. For as far back as I can remember, I've always been a daydreamer. I love making mood boards, whether physical or virtual, and then sitting back in a very relaxed state of mind and visualizing what my life will look like as I achieve each dream on my list. For me, this type of activity has an extremely calming effect on my daily life, and it's an activity I turn to time and time again. What do you have to lose, other than an erratic state of mind by doing this? When I have something on my list, I simply love feeling the feelings of satisfaction when that dream will, no doubt, be manifested into my life. In fact, studies have shown that visualizing how something feels before you physically possess it has a uniquely high energy vibration. It releases serotonin into your system. And who doesn't want more of that good-feeling high on a regular basis? Visualize what you want to attract to your life and then sit back and enjoy the feelings of already having it; it will do you a world of good in the process.

If I've said it before, I apologize, but I will say it again: *I love Oprah Winfrey.* I regularly check what books she has mentioned on her Book Club list so that I can read them as well. I've read many of her publications and always take away so many nuggets that go on to enhance my life. I love everything that she embodies and everything that she strives to teach humanity. For me, she is an incredible example of how you can manifest the life you want. I've heard her life story many times, and although parts have been riddled with pain and disappointment, she still rose above it all to create the life she wanted. She is also one of the biggest modern supporters of the law of attraction.

I had heard of this law many times in my life, but I never truly connected with it until I took a twenty-one-day online meditation course from Oprah and Deepak Chopra centered around harnessing the law of attraction in your life. My eyes were opened wide, and I immediately started using everything I learned in that twenty-one-day journey to my advantage. Once put into practice, I started noticing all of the things that were changing dramatically in my life. I would like to share the changes I noticed with you so you will better know when the law has started to work in your favor.

Change 1

I became less resistant to change. Change is the only constant. I know we've probably all heard that before. It's true; we are constantly changing, evolving, and growing. When you embrace this fundamental truth, there will no longer need to be a reason or purpose for resisting change. When we are in a place of resisting, it's usually because we can't let go of something that has happened in the past. What we don't always realize is that by resisting change, you will continue to attract that energy into your life. If the law of attraction has taught me nothing else, it's that whatever I put my energy into resisting, I'm just attracting more of that resistance to my life. Embrace the knowledge that change happens for a reason; that reason is to usually clear out negative things, experiences, and people in your life so that you have more space to accept positive things, experiences, and people into your life.

Change 2

I started sleeping much better. Being able to fall asleep and stay asleep much more easily was of great comfort to me. It was a definitive signal that I was going to bed with a much calmer mind and peaceful heart. I found that the more I embraced the law of attraction, I had less trouble falling asleep because I wasn't running the gauntlet and letting my out-of-control mind keep me up at night. When you find that you are falling asleep faster and staying asleep more consistently, welcome that. It means you are getting more comfortable with letting the law of attraction take over in your life and that you have decided to focus on pursuing your passions and true happiness. When you do this, there are far fewer things to keep you up at night.

Change 3

I became clearer on what I wanted in life. This was such a gratifying experience for me. When I became comfortable talking to and flowing with the universe, all of the clutter started to disappear more and more. I could see my goals, passions, and objectives much more clearly on a day-to-day basis. Feeling this created this sort of fervor to want to pursue my connection to the universe even more. The added bonus that I'm still discovering is that when you are accepting of flowing with the universe, you are putting out very powerful energy that grants an open door for the universe to continue working in your life.

Change 4

I felt happier and more focused on the present moment. Remember, with the law of attraction, like attracts like. So if you spend a majority of time focused on what's not going so well in your life, then guess what! You will continue to attract more people and experiences to be sad about. Likewise, if you give the majority of your focus to what is going well, you will start to attract more things that go well in your life. I also learned that you can't attract the past or the future; you can only attract in the present moment. When I got out of the habit of trying to control the past or forecast the future, I was then existing in a place of complete peace and resolve that my life would go in the direction that I would create.

Change 5

My intuition was on fire. As I started becoming more and more comfortable putting the law into practice, I absolutely experienced an increased sense of discernment or just a feeling of knowing. This has been a very comforting feeling for me. Much like the video game analogy from the opening of this chapter, I could know and see more clearly obstacles that presented themselves, no matter how the landscape had changed; this allowed me to level up much faster and go on to new and exciting levels in the game of my life. I also started to experience much more symbiosis with the universe and good things just keep coming my way. This was, without a doubt, proof positive that the law of attraction is always there. It's just a question of how I would choose to plug into it.

Change 6

I started living the life I'd always dreamed. Once I had tuned into the frequency that would propel my life forward in phenomenal ways, things sort of spiraled out of control in a very good way. I started manifesting my dreams and desires at a much faster pace. My intentions were incredibly focused. I learned to hold the positive frequency that I was broadcasting out to the universe in the forefront of my mind on a daily basis. As I continued to build momentum in this practice, I started noticing that my life just felt exponentially more whole.

I've had the best time with my friend Luis by my side. I've paid close attention to how he has traveled the road to realizing his dreams.

He's taught me so much along the way, whether he knew it or not. As with anything in life, tapping into the power that lies within the law of attraction isn't going to happen overnight. It will take effort, concentration, and being mindful to change your habits so that you find the room for this powerful universal gift to start working in your life.

I realize that the law of attraction has many complexities. I encourage you to find the best way for it to begin working in your life. For me, the most powerful reminder has been the use of *I am* statements that I review as part of my morning routine. As I'm reading these statements, I make sure to feel the intention behind them and concentrate on the feeling of satisfaction because, whether or not, they already physically exist in my life; I know that they are not far away. Here is a list of my favorites. Feel free to use them as they are or as inspiration in creating your own list.

> *I am unbounded awareness.*
> *I am healthy.*
> *I am wise.*
> *I am compassionate.*
> *I am grateful.*
> *I am welcoming abundance.*
> *I am a perfect partner.*
> *I am becoming.*
> *I am enough.*
> *I am forgiving.*
> *I am satisfied.*
> *I am honest.*
> *I am love.*
> *I am worthy.*
> *I am a magnificent creation.*

These statements bring me so much joy on a daily basis. They have the ability to center me and my intentions, and they serve as constant reminders of what I want my life to be and the person I want to be in that life. Create your list, keep it close by, read it often, and watch the law of attraction come alive for you.

$\mathcal{A}$ $\mathcal{D}$ecisive $\mathcal{L}$egend

You teach people how to treat you by what you
allow, what you *stop*, and what you *reinforce*.

—Tony Gaskins

SOMETIMES, A GREAT friendship has to suffer a great ending, even if that ending is only temporary. When I decided to say goodbye to one of the best friendships, if not the greatest friendship of my life, the decision was made with complete confidence and total abandon; it's just what I had to do.

When I moved from Georgia to Virginia in 2004, I had a head full of dreams. I had left everything I'd known in the pursuit of those dreams. I had already solidified a few friendships in Virginia in previous years, so the transition to a new environment and new way of life seemed much less daunting. I didn't know it was a mistake at the time, but I moved to Virginia with my cousin who would prove very quickly to be completely unreliable and financially unstable. We rented an apartment in one of the most popular neighborhoods of downtown Norfolk. This apartment was way outside of our means, but we were young and still in the place of making very naive decisions. We were in the apartment for a total of three months before I realized this wasn't going to work, so I moved in with a couple of friends that I had known for a few years.

Living in my new home, I initially felt completely safe and grounded. My housemates, for all I knew, were great people who had my best interest at heart. They gave me a place to call home, and I was happy. Now that I was officially settled, or so I thought, I decided it was a great time to start on the road to accomplishing my dream.

I started my apprenticeship to become a hairdresser and instantly fell in love with connecting with clients and doing anything and everything I could to make them see the beauty in themselves. I was excited to learn a new skill and ended up learning even more valuable lessons and skills in the process. Despite my family's advice against pursuing my vision, I quickly discovered that I would be more than okay following this long-felt passion of mine.

Back at home, I started noticing things that just didn't add up and that made me increasingly uncomfortable. I couldn't explain it at the time, but I've come to know that, for some reason, I was being watched, albeit my actions were being recorded on a daily basis, and I still don't know why. My housemates had ended their relationship, and now, I was living in the house with a guy that just couldn't be trusted. Of course, to my face, he showed an incredible amount of support and encouragement, but behind that facade, something much more sinister was happening, but that's a story for another day. After two years, I became so uncomfortable living in that environment; an environment where all of my lifelong friends no longer recognized me that I called another friend in the area and asked for permission to move in with him at the end of 2007.

Little did I know at the time, but Derrell would become the father I will always need, the brother I missed out on earlier in life, and the friend I will, no doubt, always be able to count on. I had met him before in many group gatherings and always loved his energy. He wasn't a pretender at all. He didn't speak that often, but when he did, for me, his words always carried great weight.

Over the next three years, we had such an incredible time together as roommates. We would pass hours together sharing experiences and him imparting his wisdom, and although most times it was not requested, it was nonetheless greatly appreciated.

When the opportunity presented itself to become an educator for a new hair care brand that hit the scene in a big way, Derrell was so happy for me. He understood my vision wasn't to work in a salon for the rest of my life but to be able to inspire and teach other people in the industry on how to be the most passionate and satisfied in their own lives. It didn't take long for the company to take notice of my innate ability to unify people and really encourage them to step out of their comfort zones and become all they were destined to be, whether in their salon or in their total experience of life. Roughly six months after becoming a regional educator, I was offered a position to come aboard full time with them, and that created the opportunity for me to move across the country, start a new role, and a new life in Seattle.

Suffice it to say, the dynamic of the friendship between Derrell and I shifted significantly. He didn't seem so happy about this new opportunity for me, and in many ways, he went out of his way to discourage the move. I remember struggling to find a balance between being so excited for such a huge opportunity and his persistent discouragement. I've come to understand in recent years, as I've gotten older, that his first instinct was to protect me, as he always had, and unfortunately, it just came across at that time as being overbearing and trying to tell me how to live my life. I've also come to understand about myself that the biggest way to get me to move out of your life is to attempt to tell me how to live, what decisions to make, and who you think I should be.

In November of 2010, we packed a small number of belongings into my car and set off on the road trip from Virginia to Seattle. We had calculated it would take us three days if we stopped only when necessary to refuel and to sleep. I have so many fond memories of that trip. Derrell and his partner Brandon had never seen the northern part of the country. We stopped to see Mount Rushmore and a few other sights along the way. It was truly an incredible three days on the road. Derrell had no idea that this trip held even more significance for me because it was on this trip that I was silently saying goodbye to our friendship. I didn't know if we would ever speak again, and that thought hurt a great deal, but I just knew deep inside that I had to cut ties and move in the direction that my soul was taking me. For me, I simply couldn't allow his overbearing nature in my life during this transitional moment, and as I dropped them off at the airport to catch their return flight to Virginia, I decided I had to stop all contact. In hindsight, I should have been brave enough to tell my friend how I was feeling, but selfishly, I made the silent decision to cut all ties and move on with my life.

I grew up being taught to be a people pleaser at all costs, so this was an enormous leap for me. When Derrell returned to Virginia, he reached out regularly, and I responded at first but slowly started to create distance between us. Distance, he no doubt, picked up on very quickly. After several weeks of reaching out with no response from me, he informed me that he was also happy to let the friendship go if that's what needed to happen for me to be happy. I remember I didn't even have the courage to respond to that message; I just let it go, and our friendship completely disappeared.

It took more than several years for us to reconnect. I remember sitting in my apartment in Phoenix, my new home on New Year's Eve 2016, and I mustered up the courage to reach out to him. I had missed him, his advice, and his friendship so much over the years. Although I had cultivated new and great friendships, his influence in my life was definitely missing. I'm not sad that I had to do it alone for so many years because those experiences taught me so much about myself; things I probably wouldn't have learned had Derrell been around protecting me and making my choices for me.

It only took a few moments for him to respond, and it blew my mind that we were able to reconnect so quickly, have the difficult conversation about what happened from each other's perspective, then quickly let it go and move forward. We started connecting more regularly, definitely with some trepidation because neither of us wanted to be hurt again. After a short time, he visited me in Arizona, and I've made multiple trips to Virginia to spend time with him and Brandon. For me, the friendship today is far above and beyond what I could have imagined for us. It's helped me grow and definitely helped him grow as well. We laugh now when he starts dispensing advice and then quickly course corrects by saying things like, "Oops,

I'm sorry. I better shut my mouth, or I will lose you for another seven years."

Keep in mind, this decision for me was not easy at all. Saying goodbye to such a great friend was a very difficult decision to make; however, I don't regret that decision. It's made me into the person that I am today, and it's brought me to a place where I'm much better at making and owning my decisions that will continue to push me toward the life I want to experience. Above all else, that reconnection experience with my friend taught me so much, and it helped me identify definite advantages to being decisive, and I'm happy to share what I've learned with you.

Decisiveness Tip 1

Conserve physical and emotional energy. Toiling over and over in making a decision is exhausting. Studies have shown that this kind of constant up and down has a significant impact on your physical and emotional wellbeing. This type of physical and emotional stress, if gone unchecked, can ultimately result in disease. Being more decisive goes a long way in eliminating anxiety, and it actually gives a boost to your self-confidence. Simply put, it's far better to set time aside when a decision needs to be made. Make sure this time is undistracted so that you make the best decision possible. Weigh the pros and cons of your decision and, when you are ready, make the decision. You will be much happier and have much more tranquility in your life when you do.

Decisiveness Tip 2

Don't procrastinate. Rip the bandage off. When your decision has been made, and you are completely comfortable with it in your heart, don't dillydally in communicating that decision with everyone it involves. Procrastination, if you're not totally aware, is a character trait that can imbed itself into most areas of your life. It can lead you to procrastinate on work projects and activities with your friends and family. To others, procrastination clearly communicates that you aren't prepared or organized. With personal relationships, it can also send the message that time spent with the ones you love is clearly not important to you; this can lead to the breakdown of relationships on all levels unnecessarily. With that said, don't procrastinate when making a decision, and don't procrastinate communicating your decision once it has been made. It's your life, your decision. As long as you deliver your decision with kindness and compassion for others and how it might affect them, the people who want to understand and remain in your life will do so.

Decisiveness Tip 3

Kill the illusion of control. Even in cases, where a person lives in an unbearable situation for years because of a dominant or abusive partner, this is still not true control; it is manipulation, the illusion of control—that's all. Control is a trick. The only thing we truly have control over in our lives is our happiness and the effort we put forth toward completing a task. The rest, especially the outcome, is never going to be under our control, so stop thinking you will control the outcome of any given situation. And definitely, stop thinking you will ever be able to control another person and what they choose to do with their lives. Keep your eyes on your own paper and control what you can in your life to make it the best life possible.

Decisiveness Tip 4

Eliminate biased inferences. We all tend to decide who someone is, usually based on past experience, and then react to them based on that decision. Unfortunately, this cuts out the possibility of us ever learning something new about them until we make a new decision. For example, when someone hurts you and giving the benefit of the doubt, it was truly an accident, we use that one incident to form a biased opinion about that person. We assume because they hurt us once, they will continue to hurt us; this is a true and unfortunate block to a flourishing relationship. Examine the circumstances, see all possibilities, and then make a new decision so that you can move forward. It is true that hurt people usually hurt other people. That doesn't mean that one instance of hurt will automatically amount to that person hurting you for a lifetime. Talk with the person that hurt you and then decide if the relationship is worth repairing. Whatever decision you make, own it and then move forward with peace of mind.

Decisiveness Tip 5

Keep or burn the bridges. Unfortunately, there are times in life when you have come to a crossroads in a relationship with another person or a job, and you have to make the decision to move forward with them or move away from them entirely; this is a tough one, and it's going to hurt no matter which decision you make.

If you decide that the relationship or job should move forward, then it will most likely necessitate some very painful and awkward conversations to get everyone involved on the same page. If your decision is to move forward, then be completely open with the other person surrounding the things that make you uncomfortable or that are causing you pain. Be kind, but don't hold back. Communicate openly and with grace so that they can really see and hear where you are coming from. Likewise, do the same for the other person when it's their turn to speak. After everyone has spoken, work on a plan together that would prevent you from getting to this place again. This will most definitely involve the creation of some healthy boundaries for which both of you are required to be accountable. In the long run, the decision you've made will hopefully make the relationship stronger, and it will continue to flourish. Just keep the boundaries in check, and you are well on your way to a happier future together.

If you decide that the relationship is something you no longer want to be a part of, the conversation could be very short or very lengthy. Here, it's still important to communicate your boundaries up front and very clearly. In most cases, the other person is going to be caught off guard, hurt, and relatively angry. Since it's your decision to move away from the relationship, I highly recommend that you speak first. Let them know the reasons you are ending the relationship and then communicate your boundaries kindly but boldly. If, in your heart of hearts, you know it's time for the relationship to end, you can either let them speak their mind or not. It's your decision; however, in light of the relationship you both shared, it would be the kind and gracious thing to do. With that said, you don't need to voluntarily become their punching bag in the process. Yes, they are going to be hurt; you're going to hurt too, but if your decision is to separate, then own that decision and move through the conversation with as much grace as you can. If they hurl insults and say really mean things, you don't have to return the favor. Kindness and taking the high road in these situations will always prevail, and it will always leave you with greater solace in the end.

I'm so happy the bridge between Derrell and I wasn't burned. Thankfully, we found our balance as friends and, in turn, became lifelong confidants. We had a strong relationship before, no doubt, but we've now moved into a mutual appreciation and respect for one another that has gone on to form an unbreakable and kindred relationship.

In recent years, we've visited each other regularly. We've shared the ups and downs of daily life. He gives me the space to breathe and make my own decisions, as hard as that may still be for him. I've also been given the added bonus of a dear and lifelong friendship with his partner Brandon in the process. Derrell is still there to guide me and give advice, but now, he lets me fall if I need to, and he is there to pick me up, dust me off, and encourage me to get back on the path to achieving my dreams. He has been one of my biggest champions in all aspects of my life, and that support is invaluable.

There have been many times in my life where I've reflected back on our experiences together. Those experiences have become a solid measuring ground for how I approach many situations in my life today. Derrell was there when I decided to buy my first home. He was there when I was noticing how frustrated I was in my work. And ultimately, he was there cheering me on when I decided to leave my job in pursuit of something better.

Making decisions in life is a responsibility that will never go away, so you might as well use the tools you have to weigh the pros and cons and then move forward and make the best decisions you possibly can. At the end of the day, I've learned that no one can make your decisions for you. I've also learned that out of the toughest situations, there can come a day when you end up with a relationship that is far better than you could have ever imagined.

My advice to all of you is to make your decisions; own them. Then, simply walk forward with compassion for all and, ultimately, with total peace of mind.

A Detached Legend

Your peace is more important than driving yourself crazy trying to understand why something happened the way it did. Let it go.

—Mandy Hale

I HAVE NO interest in fame. I have absolutely no interest in notoriety. I find things most people assign value to be extremely mundane. I do, however, hold incredible value for relationships. The idea of that elusive "best friend" is something that haunts my desires to this very day. Maybe it's because I never had the big brother role model growing up. I'm still not entirely sure; however, my quest continues to find understanding and solace with all relationships that come into and go out of my life.

I want to tell this story; rather, I need to tell this story. It's for my own personal healing. It's a story that is incredibly raw and, to a degree, still carries a lot of pain, but I've learned that we all must travel through that pain to get to a place of comfort and ease. This will be the first time I've ever written about this enormous area of struggle in my life, and my grandest hope is that it helps you and me to truly find peace in the midst of detaching from someone or something that no longer benefits your life. Even though this story is about a platonic friendship in my life, I hope you can find ways to use it to detach from any form of relationship that isn't doing you and your incredible life justice.

My story and biggest lesson about detachment starts here, followed by the techniques and tools I've found extremely valuable when you've decided you must let go of someone and move on with your life.

Not long ago, I lost one of the very best friends I've ever had. And with that loss, I've experienced such cavernous levels of pain and suffering, more than I ever remember experiencing before. I know that it's a wound that will take a considerable amount of time to heal, and still, although I now know it's not necessarily healthy, I will always remain hopeful that this incredible friend will find a way to return to my life. However, I somehow feel in the deepest parts of my being that a relationship with him on any level could always prove to be a perpetual disappointment. For me, without a doubt, it was a friendship that, from the very start, was mostly one-sided. Out of respect for him, I want to make it abundantly clear that this is my side of the story based on my experience and my feelings.

Joe and I met in 2010, and it was an instant and kindred connection for me. We seemed to share so many of the same interests, so it was very easy to give him complete access to my life immediately. It wasn't a typical friendship that develops over time; it literally developed overnight for me.

Over the course of the next six years, we were inseparable. We, or in hindsight, maybe just I, found every way possible to be able to work on projects together in our professional roles. Whenever work would take me to his city, I always stayed in his home with his wife and son. I think back on those memories with great fondness and admiration. He and his wife exhibited so many of the qualities of a stable and happy relationship, and from the first moment we were introduced officially, his wife, Molly, and I clicked even more instantly than Joe and me. They've visited and spent time with me in Arizona where I live. They taught me how to ice skate. Molly and I both share an equal love for cooking. We've had so many heartfelt conversations over the years and shared many wonderful moments together as the *three amigos*. I will always hold and cherish many fond memories of our connection and be grateful for everything that connection taught me and who it has ultimately led me to be today.

For as long as I've known him, Joe has always been an incredibly stoic person. I can only recall a couple of occasions where he let his feelings show, and I was in no way prepared for those eruptive and incredibly painful displays. In the fall of 2017, while I was visiting him and his family, I witnessed firsthand a side of him that, although encouraging to see him finally open up and show his feelings, I truly never want to have that experience again with anyone.

We had been working on a few projects that day, and for the most part, he had been very quiet and standoffish; a sign I had come to recognize and knew that it was best to just let him be because, even if I asked, there was little to no chance that he would tell me what was bothering him. Early that evening, and because they shared a vehicle, we decided it was time to finish up our work and head downtown to pick Molly up from work. We went inside her store to look around and wait on her to finish up so that we could go and prepare dinner.

Molly finally came out, and she was with her boss. She introduced him to me, and he said, "Oh, wow, it's nice to finally meet the person that Molly is always talking about so much. She talks about you all the time." In that moment, you could literally feel Joe completely shut down and start boiling with rage on the inside. I remember taking just a few steps back because his pain and anger were so palpable. The conversation with her boss was very short, and then we made our way back to the car with absolutely no words spoken between the three of us.

Finally, in the car on the way back to their house, it didn't take long for things to completely spiral out of control. Before I knew what was happening, they were both screaming at each other. In those extremely awkward moments, I remember wanting to be anywhere but inside that car. When we stopped at a traffic light, and the argument had reached its climax, Molly jumped out of the car and started walking. This led to Joe turning off the car in the middle of traffic and jumping out to chase after her. I had no idea what to do, sitting in traffic with the cars behind us blowing their horns and becoming more irate with each passing moment.

After what seemed like hours, but was really only several minutes, they were both back in the car, and we were driving back to their house. Not a word was spoken by anyone.

Back at their house, they retreated to their bedroom, shut the door, and continued their heated debate. He was hurling accusations that suggested Molly and I had something physical going on the side. I could hear Joe saying so many things to her that we all knew couldn't possibly be true. I could hear Molly defending herself and even defending me, all while trying to ensure him that nothing like that could or would ever happen. She was trying to get him to understand that we were just really close friends, and that's why she spoke about me so much to her boss.

I didn't have any idea how long their argument would continue, so I did the only rational thing. I started packing my things and looking for available hotel rooms online. In those frantic moments, I remember feeling isolated, betrayed, bewildered, and angry, and so many red flags about the history of our entire friendship flooded my mind like a dam collapsing that I couldn't possibly process them at all. Why was this happening? Didn't he trust me completely? Didn't he trust her? Hadn't I proven how noble of a friend I was over the years?

Things finally quieted down, I heard their bedroom door open, and within seconds, Molly was standing in my bedroom.

"What are you doing?" she inquired.

Through a multitude of tears, I replied, "Molly, I don't know what I'm doing here. I don't know why something like this is happening. I've done nothing wrong. Neither have you. All I know is I don't feel comfortable staying here any longer. I'm scared."

"You aren't going anywhere. You're going to stay here tonight, and we can work this out in the morning," she affirmed.

I trusted her, so I agreed to stay and see how things would be in the morning. I unpacked my belongings, shut the door, and tried to sleep. Sleep never came. I tossed and turned that night with so many questions. Had our friendship ever been true? Why was I investing so much in a person for them to easily distrust me? I was missing some crucial information, and I wasn't sure when that information would come. Little did I know, I would gain a little more clarity the next morning and ultimately realize his explosion had nothing to do with me or her. It was something raging inside of him that I still haven't come to fully understand.

I awoke the next morning after just a couple of hours of sleep and went to the kitchen to make some coffee. The house was quiet, and I made as little noise as possible to prevent waking them. When I sat down at the kitchen table to enjoy the latte, their bedroom door opened, and I could see Joe coming down the hallway to the kitchen. We didn't make eye contact because you could tell emotions were still very raw at that moment. He sat down and slowly started talking.

"Morning, Bubs," he started.

"Morning," I replied.

"I'm sorry about everything yesterday and especially last night. I was quiet yesterday because I was in my head about you and Molly being so close, and it was making me feel weird. Not because I don't trust you. I do. I know that nothing physical or romantic would or could ever happen between you two," he explained.

"You're absolutely right about that. I'm not sure how you could even imagine it as a possibility. Molly and I are very close friends, and that's because you introduced us. Otherwise, we would have never met. She's like the sister I never had. That's all," I said.

"I know that. I'm not sure why I went to such a dark place last night, but it's what her boss said that set me off, and it angered me and made me feel so insecure. But it wasn't because I thought something was happening between you and her," he continued.

"Then what was it? You had a complete meltdown. I've never experienced that before with you, so it definitely caught me off guard and made me really question everything about our friendship. What caused all of that?" I asked.

"It's hard to say, and I know it's going to sound really weird, but I wasn't mad for the reason you think I was. I was mad because when her boss said that about her talking about you all the time, in my mind, I wasn't happy because I don't want to share your friendship with anyone else. You're my best friend, and I don't want to share that with anybody else, not even her," he explained.

The conversation continued for about an hour, and in those moments, I learned things I had never known about him. I learned that he had a best friend growing up that had committed suicide, and I don't think that trauma has ever healed for him. I also learned that he's very protective and doesn't like to share. He thought that by me being such good friends with his wife that he was somehow losing me like he lost his childhood best friend, just in a different way. I wish I could tell you that this situation culminated in a happy ending and made us stronger friends than before. Sadly, it didn't. A few days later, I traveled home with a great deal of pain in my heart and not really sure about what the future would hold for our friendship. I was, however, sure that at the end of that trip, a fracture had formed in our relationship. A fracture, that to this day, still hasn't been openly discussed, mended, or healed.

Over the next couple of years, we still worked together on projects here and there, but the connection just wasn't as strong as it had been. On several occasions, I broached the subject of the disconnect I could feel only to be met with adamant resistance to an open conversation from him. So as more and more time passed, the divide increased, and the conversations slowly started to dwindle.

In the late part of 2019, and due to some organizational changes in our company, Joe and a few other employees were let go. When I got the news, I was on a holiday in the Dominican Republic with two of my friends, and I was in total shock. I reached out to him immediately to talk but was only met with a closed door. In his short response, he explained that there was nothing to talk about and that he just needed to accept what happened and move on with his life.

I couldn't believe it was so easy for him to completely close the door on a ten-year friendship. I, of course, knew he was in pain, but I truly believed our connection was much stronger and could survive anything. Over the next year, I reached out regularly to check on him, and sometimes, he would respond with another cold message—not wanting to talk, and most other times, no response to my outreach ever came. From a place of compassion, I've tried to understand his side. Maybe he thought I had some knowledge of his termination in advance and didn't give him a heads up. Maybe it was just the final straw for him, and it allowed him a quick escape from a friendship he never truly wanted. I'm not sure, I will ever know the answer.

This experience for me was crushing, and I'm positive it is one of those life-altering experiences that I will always remember and will continue to search for lessons in it. What I've learned, though, above all else is this: in life, I'm not always going to get to tell my side of the story. I've also learned from the Buddhist theology that a lie is still a lie, even if everyone believes it, and the truth is still the truth, even if no one believes it. I've come to accept and put into practice one of my newly adopted core beliefs: my peace isn't worth driving myself crazy trying to figure out why something happened the way it did. My only responsibility is to accept what is and *let it go*!

With that in mind, I started researching practical ways to completely detach from something or someone that is no longer meant to be in my life. The search for wisdom and peace has taken me across many of the world's theologies and scriptures, and I have now arrived at a place, after practicing these precepts, that I can share them with you in what is, hopefully, a more digestible format. So let's get started breaking attachments that are no longer leading us to the life we truly want to experience.

One: Detachment Is Painful

Understandably so, deciding to detach from something or someone that you have poured a great amount of energy into is going to be painful at first. Moving away from anything or anyone when you have dedicated your time, love, and affection can almost always feel like you are removing a part of your body. The amount of pain you feel is in direct proportion to the amount of time you have spent building that attachment. Creating this type of tie takes time, and the more time spent building attachments, the more ties you are creating between you and the object of your attachment. Even though letting go of something feels painful, it's building attachments in the first place that are the true source of the pain. All of the bonds created through attachment prevent you from being truly free and the person you actually are.

Two: Attachment Is Conditional Love

Finding a way to detach from the things and people that hold you back opens you up to the ability to love unconditionally. If the person in your life only shows you love when you please them, build them up, do what they want when they want, then they are definitely attached to you; deciding to love you when you meet their conditions and just as easily deciding to withhold that love when you don't measure up to every expectation that they have of you. This goes both ways. If you are treating another person the same way, then you are attached to them. You both deserve to be free, and it's your vital task to recognize these patterns in your life that lead to codependent relationships or habits and decide to detach from them as quickly as you possibly can.

Three: Attachment and Self-Worth Are Not Friends

The more you are attached to someone or something, the more it becomes a defining source of your self-worth. If your self-worth is predominantly defined through attachments to people and things, I implore you to break free as soon as possible because it's not who you actually are inside. Of course, we all want to surround ourselves with great people, and we want to live in a beautiful home and have nice things. But if you *need* any of those things to feel valued and wanted, then you are attached, and those are the things that are building a mental picture of your self-worth. But the only source of your self-esteem has to come from inside you, not from anything or anyone outside of you. Become detached in this aspect of your life in order to experience the person that you actually are. That person deep inside is the best version of you there ever will be.

Four: Attachment Is a Trap

I'm sure we've all seen a spider building a web in our lifetime. Think of attachments like that. The spider spends a great deal of time and energy constructing its web and making sure every strand of the web connects and that it's solid, practically unbreakable. We all, from time to time, have built these same types of webs in relationship to other people, things, and habits. We have done this for the most part unconsciously, and because of this, it's a lot easier for us to fall into the trap of being attached to people and things and ideas far more often because we aren't paying the necessary attention. Examine your life and identify the places where you have created "spider webs" to other people and things and work diligently to break those bonds that can ensnare you every single time.

Five: Attachment Is Needy

This aspect is directly related to your relationships with other people. We are all created with the common goal of connecting to other human beings. We are social creatures and building solid relationships based on mutual trust, support, and freedom to live the life you want is a fundamental need. However, when we attach our emotions to other people, we can get way off track from authentic human interaction. The best way to identify if you are attached to other people is to look around your circle. Do you need someone else to make you feel happy, make you feel loved and appreciated, and make you feel valuable in the world? If so, then you are giving others total power and control over your experience of life. The only person you truly *need* in life is *you*. You are the source and creator of your experience, so please trust that you are enough in all things and enough when around all people. Of course, spend time with others that you love unconditionally and that love you unconditionally in return. But also, make time to spend time alone so that you get to experience the incredible person that you are!

Letting go of something or someone is going to cost you. I don't want to mislead anyone and make them think that detaching from something that no longer serves your life is going to be an overnight occurrence; it's not. It will take time and dedication to break bonds that you have spent so much time constructing. It's going to cost you relationships and being understood by people, but what you have to lose is minuscule compared to what you have to gain through your decision to detach.

The only legitimate things you have to lose from letting go of something or someone are things and people that were built for the person you no longer are and the person you definitely won't be moving forward. You can still, however, stand strong in the knowledge that the people and things that are truly meant for your life will all meet you on the other side of this transformation.

The things that you have to gain always inspire me and motivate me to break the bonds that no longer serve me and the life I want to lead. Firstly, you will get to construct a new comfort zone suited exactly to your liking. You will start to transition to a place in your relationships where you won't be just liked, you will be loved. You won't just be understood, you will be truly seen.

It's also going to feel incredibly strange at first when you start moving in this new direction; that's because you are now taking the lead in assigning accountability to everyone including yourself for the future of all your relationships. The thing that makes accountability so hard to swallow for others is that accountability can very much feel like an attack when people aren't yet ready to recognize and take responsibility for the fact that their actions can harm other people. Still, be steadfast in your decision once you've made your mind up and continue editing your life because it's your work of art after all.

Through my greatest experience in detaching from Joe, I ended up creating six tips that helped me tremendously, and I would like to share those tips with you.

Detachment Tip 1

Beautiful boundaries. Boundaries are your line in the sand; they protect you and ultimately protect the other person from future disappointment or disillusionment concerning the relationship moving forward. Your responsibility here is to be very clear with your boundaries because people will, no doubt, learn how to treat you based on what you allow, what you stop, and what you reinforce.

Detachment Tip 2

Consciousness creates change. Once you've set your boundaries, keep them in the forefront of your consciousness. In the beginning, this may need to be a daily practice, but it will eventually become second nature. Write your new boundaries down and make sure they are easy to access for when you need that gentle reminder of what they are. When you start enforcing your new boundaries, make time to check in on yourself to see how you are feeling. When you do that, strive to be extremely conscious about what you are truly feeling so that you can move through those emotions more quickly.

Detachment Tip 3

Forgiveness forgoes frustration. Forgive as quickly and completely as you can. Forgive them and forgive yourself. When you reach a place of forgiveness for everything that happened, frustration then disappears from your life. Granted, this won't be an overnight process, but it will happen.

Detachment Tip 4

Goodbye grants gratitude. When you've made the decision to say goodbye to something or someone, *mean it*! Don't keep returning to the situation and reopening the wound; that won't do anything good for your development. Make time to be grateful for everything the experience has taught you—whether good or bad. Be grateful for the complete experience. I can guarantee that you are going to feel so amazing and so strong down the road because you have finally chosen yourself above all things, and you're the most important choice in your life. Don't ever forget that.

Detachment Tip 5

Suffering secures solace. When you have made the firm decision to detach, there will be moments, no doubt, that it's going to hurt, and sometimes—depending on the level of attachment—it's going to be incredibly painful for you. In those moments, I would encourage you to make space for the pain. Don't bottle it up or push it down inside. I've learned that by creating space for the pain to exist, you are also simultaneously creating free space to move through that pain more quickly. I've also experienced, with great appreciation, that during those painful moments, solace has a funny way of appearing; it appears and offers great comfort and brings you to a place of peace and understanding. None of this means that you will ever forget the person or the experience. It just means that you've made the solid decision that the person or thing no longer fits into the idea of what you want your life to be. That can be a temporary decision or a permanent one. You get to decide.

Detachment Tip 6

Acceptance advances awareness. Just accept everything that comes from your decision to let go: your pain, their pain, the unknown. Be okay that things change, and you are changing into something far greater than you were yesterday. Acceptance will create much more awareness in you so that you can recognize that kind of person or situation far more quickly next time, and you will choose to travel a different path because you've truly learned the lesson. Some lessons have to be learned many times. It's part of your growing process and completely normal. But when you do the work and can look down the road to your future self, you will be able to say to anyone and everyone, "If you know who I am based on the person I was a year ago, then you don't know me at all. Trust me, my growth game has been strong. Please allow me to introduce myself."

I've learned that the pain I went through after my friendship with Joe came to an end was because I completely ignored the precepts outlined above, but you don't know what you don't know, right? Now that I know these wise guidelines and have been able to incorporate them into the forefront of my consciousness, I've become more and more detached from all things that don't align with the life I want to experience moving forward. And honestly, as I continue to grow older, I've come to believe that we have the ability and the obligation to continue cultivating our circles of influence and, with that cultivation, only letting certain people in at certain times. Obviously, you continue to be open, honest, and real with everyone you meet while still understanding not everyone you encounter in life is destined to have a seat at the table of your life.

In a perfect world, one day in the not-so-distant future, my friend Joe and I will be at the same table again. It would be a great day of sharing truth, being completely open with each other, and based on history, a load of fun and more good memories to add to the bank. But until that day comes, if ever, I've decided to spend my time and energy focused on the life I want and not being attached to a story that might be destined to have no end.

8

$\mathcal{A}$ Grateful Legend

Challenges are gifts that force us to search for a new center
of gravity. Don't fight them. Just find a new way to stand.

—Oprah Winfrey

SITTING ON TOP of The Standard Hotel in Los Angeles during the fall
of 2017 will always remain as the moment where one of life's biggest
gifts and lessons was revealed to me. I had just finished a taxing day
at work, and my friend Paz and I retired to the outside lounge terrace
on the top floor of the hotel with other coworkers to wind down for
the day and enjoy an adult beverage. Everyone was having a great
time recounting the events of the day, and it wasn't long before Paz
and I sort of secluded ourselves and were both drawn into a conversation about life that is one of the best conversations I've ever had.

We've always shared a mutual language that involves no words
at all. We can simply make eye contact and have the most beautiful
conversation in the world without ever uttering a word. We have
always been able to bring out the fun in any stressful situation just
by making eye contact and then ultimately having a laugh together.

Initially, I could tell that something was troubling my dear friend,
so I asked her what was wrong; that's when I learned a large part of
her story and what has made her into the incredible person that she
is today. It's her stance on gratitude. Essentially, to Paz, the definition

of gratitude has become: to be thankful for what you have right now and the experiences or lessons that you have had with people that have left your life. Gratitude for her in large part is also compassion for yourself, to understand that things in life will be challenging sometimes, but you can always find the silver lining if you look for it hard enough. She believes that gratitude makes you appreciate everything about any environment you find yourself, good or challenging, and if you're mindful, it can lead you to find appreciation for the present moment. It may take time, but gratitude is always reachable.

In our time on the rooftop that night, I learned that the most difficult moment in her life was going through her divorce, ultimately deciding to end a marriage that she had for twelve years. She didn't have a backup plan or security to help her, but she knew it was time to stand up and make the decision to sink or swim, and because they had two children together, she had to find a way to carry on. During this major transition in her life, she wasn't sure how she was going to pay her bills or put food on the table; however, she found the strength to persevere in the eyes of her children. Through her gratitude for them, she discovered the strength that allowed her to accomplish so many things; that gratitude restored her faith in the fact that there is always a solution. It may take time to stumble onto that solution, but she now knows that things will always work out.

Her mom passed away two years before the divorce, and after it happened, she just looked at a picture of her late mother and asked, "Mom, what would you do?" and in that moment, she was filled with so much gratitude that no matter how hard the current moment is, she would get to where she wanted to be. She started waking up every day being mindful of gratitude for everything that she did have in her life. She made it a daily practice, morning and night, of being grateful before the day started and making sure to make notes on what she was grateful for at the end of each day.

Since that night in 2017, Paz and I have kept in very regular communication with each other. Her experience of great loss in her life didn't end with her divorce. Shortly after her mother died, her brother became an alcoholic—a condition that led to his divorce as well—and shortly after that major life change, he spiraled into a very dark place of abusing alcohol that ultimately took his life. Even through this, Paz had learned that her best option was to find solace and comfort in the arms of gratitude. She made a new daily practice of being grateful for all of the moments they shared so that she could effectively let him go.

As if losing her mother, going through a divorce, and then losing her brother wasn't enough for one person to endure, Paz also lost her father within two years of her brother's death. She still remembers all of her lost loved ones on birthdays and holidays. And those days, although extremely difficult, have motivated her to find gratitude in every single day because you just never know how many more moments on this earth you're going to have.

If you met Paz today, you would have no idea that she has endured such suffering and loss in her life. She is a force of positivity and light in every moment. It's that positivity and light that makes so many people want to share time with her. I'm grateful for all of the moments we've shared, and even more grateful that she has shown me just how impactful embracing a mindset of gratitude and practicing it daily can be and how it can strengthen you during the toughest storms and ultimately shape your life for the better. I've come to learn through my dear friend that if you can cultivate an attitude of gratitude in the following life experiences, then you are setting yourself up to lead a more fulfilled and satisfying life.

Gratitude Through Loss

Loss could be losing something material like a job, house, car, you name it, or something even more challenging like losing someone, whether that's a relationship of any kind breaking apart or, much more difficult, losing someone to death. Loss is no doubt a challenging and heart-wrenching life experience, so I want to give the utmost respect to this topic and offer absolute support and encouragement for whatever you may be going through in terms of losing something or losing someone.

I find a lot of value and comfort in quotes written by great people that I admire. I stumbled across a quote from Dodinsky not long ago and it has helped me many times in dealing with something or someone I've lost.

Dodinsky is a *New York Times* best-selling author that wrote books like *In the Garden of Happiness* and *In the Garden of Thoughts*. He's quickly become recognized as a great thought leader on topics like self-empowerment and contentment. He said in relation to grief and sorrow, "Grieving is a necessary passage and a difficult transition to finally letting go of sorrow—it is not a permanent rest stop.".

For me, this is a perfect mindset to adopt in order to prepare us all for finding gratitude in times of loss because finding a way to be grateful for something or someone that has just been taken from your life can be extremely difficult and painful. This can make it so difficult to find ways to be grateful or even the desire to try, but I do know that it is completely possible, and once you can find gratitude during life's toughest seasons, it can really alter your thinking and perspective about so many other areas of your life.

After we experience a loss, common human behavior is to focus on what we no longer have. As a result, we put the majority of our energy on the negative, on what is missing in our life, rather than focusing on the positive; all of those amazing things and people we still have. That cycle of wanting what we don't have and, in turn, wasting what we do have can create a vicious downward spiral that wouldn't be beneficial at all. To translate that into a situation involving loss—by wanting what is no longer in our life is, in fact, in many ways, wasting what still remains in our life.

We usually don't think about giving thanks when we lose something or someone that held value in our lives, and it's not our first reaction at all when someone dies. Gratitude, however, can be one of the most healing tools we have.

Finding ways to be grateful for what remains after you have experienced a loss on any level can be a powerful way to deal with, and heal, that loss. Turning your attention to how your life was enriched because that person was in it, for example, rather than on the great void the loss created, is one extremely powerful and healthy way to confront grief.

That's the sheer magic of gratitude. Gratitude has the power to help us rise above our loss. It reaffirms the amazing life that we have. It gives us hope, and most importantly, it helps us let go of the past and focus on the abundance that surrounds us now. I would like to share some tips with you that have truly helped me cultivate a mindset of gratitude during the most difficult of life's challenges.

Loss Tip 1

Gratitude generates gentleness. When you've lost something or someone that is very important to you, it's completely normal to be angry, depressed, lonely, and really confused. This can cause your life to feel incredibly chaotic as we all know, but what I've experienced is finding a way to be grateful for the thing or person when you had it or them; it eases your tension and can put you in a place of perfect gentleness that is calm and peaceful. In that new state of mind, you can then move through the feelings of loss a lot more effectively.

Loss Tip 2

Gratitude grants grace; this is more relative to when someone has chosen to leave your life—a friend, partner, husband, or wife. When that happens, it's natural for us to feel hurt, overwhelmed, bitter, and sometimes, we may even want to strike out against them and hurt them as much as they've made us hurt by leaving. This approach, however, doesn't do anything good for them, and it certainly doesn't do anything good for you. I get it, trust me, it's hard to accept when someone chooses to leave your life, and you may never get the true answer as to why. Not having closure can be so very difficult and painful. What I've found in these situations is that finding gratitude for the lessons and experiences you had with them is a great way to build a bridge to a happier place in your life. It's not easy to let go at first, but being grateful for the time you did share will get you to the other side of that bridge where the grass is no doubt greener.

Loss Tip 3

Gratitude grasps grief. Don't feel bad about grieving. Grief is a normal human emotion, and it deserves to be felt. Don't try to push the grief aside or push it down deep within yourself. It needs to be experienced as quickly as you can allow it. Gratitude is, no doubt, a great vehicle for you to be able to grasp that grief in the forefront of your mind and emotions; let it have space to be exactly what it is, and then by finding gratitude in those moments, you are giving your grief the respect and honor it deserves so that you can move through it more quickly and more efficiently.

Loss Tip 4

Gratitude grants growth. Losing something or someone, as hard as it may be to see in the moments of pain and suffering, is an opportunity for growth. We are all always growing and changing. We all have heard before that change is the only constant in life; I truly believe that. Loss is not something that you will ever stop experiencing while you're alive. It's normal and can be a beautiful part of life once you're able to see that applying gratitude to times of loss can create a better understanding and reverence for life lessons that we are all meant to learn on our journey. Having gratitude and growing forward after a loss doesn't mean you will ever forget the person or the relationship, it just means you've decided to honor the lessons learned, have joy and happiness for the wonderful memories, and still choose to grow forward in becoming a stronger, more resilient person day by day.

Gratitude Through Uncertainty

Not being certain about the outcome of anything in life can be frustrating. We all know that change will continue to be a regular part of our experience in life, and if you're anything like me, change can bring about unease and discomfort because we won't always know what's going to happen; however, you still have a choice when faced with uncertainty. You can let the weight and idea of change crash on top of you while you fight to stay afloat, or you can choose to ride the wave of change. It's up to you.

Trust me, I get it. Change is a bitter pill to swallow sometimes because everything in your life is going just so perfectly. All the stars have aligned, and you are having such a smooth ride. Then, out of nowhere, *wham*, you get hit, knocked off your feet, and are scrambling to get back up. It can be frustrating because we tend to think the universe is now out to sabotage our hopes and dreams. The initial reaction when this happens is a very gut-level and personal response, but don't allow yourself to go to a place where you are taking change personally. The key, I've found, is in finding ways to create certainty while at the same time realizing you can't control most things in life.

Creating certainty in the things that you do have control over can help you adjust to many life events: a new city, new job, loss of a loved one, or a friendship ending. In dealing with uncertainty and searching for gratitude in the midst of it, I've developed six tips that could help you on this part of your journey.

Uncertainty Tip 1

Change creates commotion. It's normal for the level of commotion to rise when you first become aware that something is changing. Embrace that commotion and find the quickest way possible to be grateful for being upended. In that upending, you are being presented with a huge opportunity to grow.

Uncertainty Tip 2

Uncertainty unleashes unease. Again, unease can be a beautiful part of life. When you have moments of discomfort and uncertainty, wrap your arms around the experience and find comfort in the knowledge that what is coming is ultimately much better than what is gone.

Uncertainty Tip 3

Certainty causes confidence. Remind yourself on a very regular basis to be confident that change isn't the enemy. You may not have all the answers, but you can choose to just focus on the road ahead and continue moving forward.

Uncertainty Tip 4

Forget the fear. Remember that fear and actual danger are not even closely related. Danger is something that is very much happening to you or around you and deserves the appropriate fight or flight response. Fear is not real, but fear relies on you being uncomfortable during a time of uncertainty because then it can play all sorts of false dialogues and scenarios out in your head. Confront the fear, knowing full well that it isn't real.

Uncertainty Tip 5

Thoughts take away tranquility. Don't become a prisoner to your thoughts because your mind will always present so many what-if questions if you allow that to happen. Find moments of peace to remind yourself that you're completely okay, you're going to be okay, and all will work out for the best in your life.

Uncertainty Tip 6

Mindset manages melancholy. Your mindset during uncertain times or events is absolutely crucial. Give yourself regular pep talks to prevent going into a state of depression about the things that are changing around you. You can't control the changing thing, but you can absolutely control your mindset about it.

Gratitude Through Anger

The Buddha said, "Holding on to anger is like grasping a hot coal with the intent of throwing it at someone else—you are the one who gets burned." I couldn't possibly agree more with those wise words.

Anger surfaces from within us based on our individual perceptions of a person or event. When it arises specifically because of another person, it's because we have interpreted their actions or behaviors as being at least one of the following: attacking, threatening, lacking validation, ill-treatment, or disrespect. Anger can also show itself because we feel frustrated or powerless in any given situation.

Anger has a tendency to work against us. It relies on our perception or interpretation of a person and their actions. That perception or interpretation is based on something we were taught, not something that is necessarily true. Anger wastes our energy by presenting a potentially false reality to us; a false narrative that usually we then turn into a true story in our mind and proceed to replay that story over and over. It's exhausting.

Anger is a completely normal human emotion. We will be dealing with moments of anger during our life. Don't suppress it; rather, be open and honest about why you are angry to the person who made you angry in a calm and collected manner. I've come to know that finding gratitude in moments of anger is one of the best solutions to putting out the fire of your discontent. Working through anger in my own life, I've developed some tips that I hope will help you navigate this emotion that more than anything wastes your time and the energy you could be spending on something much more productive.

Anger Tip 1

Anger antagonizes animosity. Anger is the adversary, and letting that adversary continue unchecked can create more long-term animosity toward another person. Truth is, they are most likely not thinking about the situation anymore—only you are, so you are essentially tying your own hands and putting yourself in lockdown. Find gratitude so that you can become the protagonist in the midst of anger.

Anger Tip 2

Rage rejects reality. Anger creates a false dialogue in your head. It puts blinders on you so you can't see any other possibility. At the same time, it prevents you from seeing the totality of the situation from all points of view. In moments where you may feel your anger moving to a place of rage, it's highly recommended to quickly change your focus onto something else until you can return to the situation and view it objectively and with more rationale.

Anger Tip 3

Wrath weakens wisdom. Anger absolutely deserves to be felt. Create a safe space where you can analyze the emotion rather than letting it run wild. Anger running wild and free through your mind definitely elevates it to a place of wrath, and that's not a comfortable existence. It's far better to make the effort to move through the emotion consciously so that you stay out of the red zone. And in every case, no matter what the offense was, the calm, kind, and wise response will always be the better option for you and for the other person.

Anger Tip 4

Resentment raises rashness. Unaddressed anger has the ability to evolve into something far worse—resentment. When we become resentful, we tend to treat many other people in our life much more rashly. Holding onto anger ultimately can have a huge impact on all other relationships in your life. Find a way to work through the anger quickly and calmly so that it doesn't build into resentment and subsequently diminish other relationships that you love having in your life.

Anger Tip 5

Madness mitigates mindlessness. When we let anger take us into the hot zone, we are not being mindful at all; we are completely out of our minds. You know what I'm talking about here. Gratitude in these moments can shift you to being glad instead of mad. Having a grateful mindset will show you the lesson in the situation far more quickly. Once the lesson is visible, your conscious mind will lead you out of the anger.

Gratitude Through Betrayal

If you've ever been betrayed by someone that you have cared for, then you know that it's an incredibly difficult hurt to heal; that's because betrayal brings up so many different feelings all at the same time. You are confronted with broken trust. You feel completely disregarded. To a degree, you probably heap on a certain amount of self-loathing and shame because you blame yourself for missing red flags that surely would have shown you that betrayal was coming.

I want to encourage you to consider betrayal from a different viewpoint. Perhaps what the person did was the only logical choice for them. When you can see that, it's far easier to have gratitude for the lesson and then be able to offer forgiveness for the betrayal more quickly. Ruminating about what happened, suffering over it, and railing on and on about the act won't change anything. Accept that it happened and at the same time accept that you can't go back and change what took place. You can only move forward. There also might be a need to forgive yourself. Look to see if you ignored certain signs or neglected to take certain actions that might have made a difference in whatever they did. Once you can see that, forgive yourself and let it go.

Betrayal is a gut-wrenching event. I've been betrayed one time too many in my life and I've identified a few things we can recognize to help us through such a life-shifting occurrence.

Betrayal Tip 1

Losing loyalty lacerates; it cuts really deep. That's normal; however, please don't lacerate them in return. There will be no benefit for you in seeking revenge.

Betrayal Tip 2

The high road heals. Opting to take the high road will most likely not be your first choice. In some cases, the person who betrayed you may want to have a conversation about what happened. You get to decide if that conversation is something you want to have. If you do decide to talk, enter the conversation with as much grace and compassion you can muster. If you choose not to have a conversation, that is still considered taking the high road. It's far better in some cases to say nothing rather than uttering words that you won't be able to take back. In the end, taking the high road in the face of betrayal will propel you to a place where you process the hurt and pain much faster and are then able to move on more peacefully.

Betrayal Tip 3

Healing happens with healthy habits. Develop healthy habits that move you to a place of healing. Don't obsess over what happened; that will not change it at all. Healthy habits to work through the pain could be journaling about the situation, writing them a letter with no intention of actually sending it, practicing kindness and forgiveness for yourself, and searching for the lessons that will help you heal.

Every day, I'm so grateful for my friend Paz and the attitude of gratitude she has unleashed in me. Practicing gratitude has become one of my favorite daily activities. Having gratitude in the good times is far easier than in the tough and challenging moments. Regardless, I've come to understand that bringing gratitude into your life is not going to happen overnight. But as I continue to strengthen my mindset of gratitude, I've noticed that more and more opportunities to be grateful enter my life through new experiences, new people, and new ideas.

I highly recommend you strive to include gratitude as a daily practice then sit back and watch your life expand in phenomenal ways.

A Forgiving Legend

Never wish them pain. That's not who you are. If
they caused you pain, they must have pain inside.
Wish them healing. That's what they need.

—Najwa Zebian

TIME SPENT LAUGHING, and I mean truly rolling around laughing, is one of my favorite escapes. Actually, there is quite a lot of science and studies that outline the benefits of regular laughter for our mental, emotional, and physical state of being. As a matter of fact, most recent studies show that laughter on a regular basis has the following impact on your life:

> *You live longer.*
> *You give a boost to your immune system.*
> *You experience pain relief.*
> *You reduce depression.*
> *You enhance your personal relationships.*
> *You have a great internal physical workout.*
> *You improve your breathing.*
> *You lose weight.*
> *You protect your heart.*

Aside from the list above, I think we can all agree that the main motivation for laughing is that it just feels really good. Can you remember the last time you had a gut-busting round of laughter? Can you remember how you felt afterward? No matter what your life looks like right now, I strongly encourage everyone to surround themselves with people who truly make you laugh and who you can make laugh in return. Without a doubt, relationships built on great humor and consistent rounds of laughter are the relationships that I'm attracted to the most, and they are also the people that I will return to time and time again for solid human connection and, even more so, when I'm feeling less than amazing on any given day.

A large bundle of laughs is the absolute best way to describe my relationship with my friend Sandra. I can't count the number of times we have connected through laughter and how that has truly enriched both of our lives. Laughter in silly times, laughter through heartbreak, and laughter in loneliness and sad times have become the cornerstone of our friendship, and I'm so thankful. Of course, we also have had some very deep and thought-provoking conversations spanning a multitude of topics, but our friendship is ultimately grounded in the fact that we both like to laugh and then laugh some more. No matter what we may be discussing, nine times out of ten, we end up in some serious fits of laughter; these times are some of my favorites because I've been able to see the huge impact our many conversations over the years has had on my life.

I met Sandra in 2010. I was giving a training workshop to prepare a new group of hairstyling educators for their journey into becoming education leaders for the hair care brand with, which I was associated. Needless to say, Sandra made an immediate impact. She's the type of person that may, at first, seem guarded and uninterested, but I've learned over the years that's just her manner of protecting her heart and the people in her life; one of her qualities that I still hold dear to this day.

I've come to know that she is a fiercely loyal person, she loves to make people feel good, and when you have the privilege of being in her inner circle, she isn't afraid to pop your bubble when you're being ridiculous, self-critical, or traveling down a path that may be harmful for you. On many occasions, she has said to me in no uncertain terms, "Tim, you're being a bit ridiculous about this, you're better than this, you deserve better than this." At the same time, she doesn't force you to change. She just shares her opinion and wisdom and lets the universe take the lead.

Sandra is a force to be reckoned with, no doubt. For several years, we traveled together throughout Mexico working to grow our brand's visibility in a new and exciting market. We've shared so many laughs on these trips and even more laughs reminiscing about many of our experiences in Mexico. We couldn't be more opposite in terms of physical attributes. I'm a six-foot-four, thin-framed Caucasian guy with ever-so-slight ginger characteristics and a tendency to be more relaxed and tranquil as I move through my day, and Sandra is a four-foot-eleven Mexican-born female who prefers to move through her day like a tornado—all passion and fire with a strong propensity for being the late arrival to anything, no matter how important the event may be.

In the animal kingdom, we would no doubt be one of those adorable YouTube videos where a giraffe befriends a Tasmanian devil. It's no surprise, because of this, that people stop and stare whenever we are together.

We decided to start our own little book club a few years ago, and it's not shocking that we are completely different in this as well. I read way too fast for her liking, and she reads way too casually for my taste. So when we tried, on several occasions to talk about the book, we ended up laughing even more because I'm always three to four chapters ahead, ultimately ruining the reading experience for her, so our little book club still exists technically, but there is seldom if ever any attendance.

We also share an affinity for great movies, documentaries, and other series that inspire growth and change in our own lives. We've spent many hours discussing things we have learned and how we can apply those lessons to our own lives.

We both share a strong love for espresso martinis, and some of my favorite memories with Sandra is sitting on the outside terrace at our hotel in Mexico City listening to the live band and enjoying more than a few of our favorite cocktails. In those times, we have both shared tears, fears, frustrations, and truly gut-busting fits of laughter. I will always hold those memories very deep in my heart because they illustrate the importance of laughter and the positive effect it has had on my life.

During the COVID-19 pandemic that wreaked havoc on the world for most of 2020, all of my regular travel came to a sudden halt in March of that year. I had been used to traveling to faraway places on a weekly basis for ten years, and now, that all stopped. Needless to say, I experienced a huge shift in my regular routine. So it was during this time of significant transition and adjustment that I decided to renovate my house. I mean, when else was I going to have the time and opportunity to take on a project like this? I took a ten-day vacation from work, had a sixty-foot dumpster delivered to my home, and in those ten days, I pretty much gutted the interior right down to the studs. I removed all the current flooring, light fixtures, and vent covers. You name it, if it was "old," it either got repurposed, donated, or put in the dumpster. It's important to point out here that I had no previous renovation experience. My dad, when he was living, was a carpenter, so I like to think maybe some of his skills lived on in my DNA.

I can honestly say, during the renovation, I made no serious mistakes. If you count it as "not serious" when you slice through the main waterline or sanding a new desktop for about an hour before realizing that I was sanding with the cover still on the sander. Many lessons learned in that venture for sure and yet still many more laughs and tears during the journey.

This experience for me ended up being a back-breaking, inspiring, physical, and emotional journey. I noticed that the connection between physically tearing out what is "old" and replacing it with what is "new" had a direct and profound connection to my spiritual journey as well. Remember in the beginning of this book when I mentioned preparing your lunch box for the day ahead? I now had the opportunity to purposefully plan everything I was going to put in my house that would bring me tranquility and remind me to be mindful of the wonderful life I have; the wonderful life that we all have. The strongest connection and lesson this experience taught me was centered around the idea of forgiveness.

Before long, my gratitude journal that I write in a night became a forgiveness journal of sorts. As I would write and recount my day, it was a very healing experience for me to use the tasks I had done that day as a metaphor for what "old" things I could tear out from inside my spirit. I would ask myself each night, "What did I need to forgive today?"

During the early parts of the renovation process, Sandra came to visit, and, boy, did we have an amazing time. Beforehand, we had decided to do some painting, but of course, I changed the plan before she got here without telling her—one of her favorite qualities about me, no doubt. I decided we would build the desktop for my new standing desk area. Needless to say, *we had a blast!* We learned so much together, laughing the entire time literally. I learned that it's best to listen to her when she has a good idea about how we should approach a project. My stubbornness still gets the best of me to this day, but I'm working on it. I also learned that if you want something to be perfectly level, don't put Sandra in charge of holding the level. So a project that should have taken an hour max ended up taking us pretty much the entire day.

A few days later, Sandra returned to San Diego, and one night shortly after, we were on the phone talking and laughing about our little desk project, she said that she was sending me something in the mail that she hoped I would like. About a week later, I received a book in the mail titled *Left to Tell—Discovering God Amidst the Rwandan Holocaust* by Immaculée Ilibagiza with Steve Erwin; this book, I would find out, is all about forgiveness. As I started to read, my hair started to stand up on end. How was it that Sandra knew I was having an internal awakening around forgiveness? Oh, the universe has strange ways of delivering exactly what you need when you are truly open and moving toward radical change in your life.

I couldn't put the book down. I read it from cover to cover in about three days. I highly recommend anyone to read that book because after Immaculée experienced horror beyond my wildest comprehension during the genocide that crippled Rwanda, she still had such a strong connection to the power of forgiveness and how it can propel your life forward or, if you choose not to forgive, how it can and will keep you stuck in your life.

The story and lessons from that book were still resonating strongly with me for several days after. One night, as I was writing in my new forgiveness journal, something hit me like a strong wave. My spirit sat up at full attention as I began to unpack another incredibly valuable lesson about forgiveness. Remember, my desk project with Sandra and how a project that should have taken an hour took almost the entire day? The universe was now whispering directly to my spirit and saying:

Tim, this is exactly how forgiveness works. Don't get frustrated because you imagine that forgiving someone or a situation should be a quick fix. It's not always going to be that easy. This is major spiritual work and a process that will take time. Just like you didn't build the desk in the time frame you thought was appropriate, you also won't always be able to forgive completely in the timeframe that you think is appropriate. Give yourself a break, don't take it personally, and don't set unrealistic goals around forgiveness for yourself. You will get there, just believe and trust the process. Also, realize that forgiveness is not about the other person at all. That's where we all get stuck. You say, 'I'm not going to forgive so-and-so because they hurt me so bad or they disappointed me, and I will never trust them again.' Listen to me, forgiveness is totally and completely about you and only you. You will not move forward if you don't forgive because you are the one, the only one responsible for putting yourself in prison. Be kind to yourself. What have you got to lose from forgiving someone and ultimately letting yourself be free?

That was such a freeing experience for me. I slept so well that night, and the next day, I started researching the topic of forgiveness and how I could apply it to my life immediately. Here is what I found to be fundamentally true and lasting for me, and I hope it helps you to start your own journey toward total forgiveness. The concepts below are a constant reminder for me when I'm struggling with forgiveness, and they serve as a roadmap of reminders that ultimately help me work through the stages of forgiveness so that I can be completely free.

1. First and foremost, forgiveness is not about the other person at all. I know it seems that way, but forgiveness is only about you and ensuring you aren't tying yourself up in a self-imposed prison.

2. Forgiveness doesn't mean you have to continue a relationship with the person you are forgiving.

3. When forgiving others, make sure you take time to forgive yourself as well.

4. Forgiveness doesn't mean forgetting the lesson you learned.

5. Forgiveness will take time. It's not something that can always be accomplished in a matter of minutes. It takes practice.

6. Forgiveness is not an act of a weak person. It's actually the exact opposite. Forgiveness strengthens you from within because it's one of the best acts of self-love you can give to yourself.

7. It's much easier to forgive when you find a way to shift your consciousness to a place that allows you to realize that anyone who offends you or hurts you oftentimes doesn't do so on purpose. None of us were born with the nature to hurt others. We've all learned that from someone or multiple people as we grow up. If you can see them as being taught to be that way, it's a lot easier, in my experience to move to a place of having more compassion for them, which ultimately leads to forgiveness.

One of the best activities surrounding forgiveness I have ever done and continue to do to this day is writing a letter to the person I want to forgive, reading the letter out loud, tearing up the letter into pieces, and then placing the torn letters into a container which I then light on fire and watch the papers burn to ash. For me, it's such a powerful experience. I've done it along the way with a few friends that have visited, and they admitted it was such a powerful release as well. I got this letter from a book that I can't honestly remember the book's name, and it has worked perfectly for me every time I feel I haven't forgiven someone. I've outlined the letter below in the hopes that it will be a new tool for you to become more and more forgiving in your life. It truly does set you free.

A Letter on Forgiveness

Dear (insert person's name),

    I forgive you for (list the things that come to your mind).
    I want to thank you for all the gifts you have given me to make me into the magnificent person that I am. I love you and apologize for not accepting you exactly as you are.

                            Love,
                  (put your name here)

When I've done this activity, it never fails that the hardest letter I have to write is the letter forgiving myself. It brings up so much emotion but, again, is such a life-giving experience. So please, whatever you do, don't forget to write a letter of forgiveness to yourself.

I'm also a big fan of collecting life-affirming quotes to help me in my journey, especially with forgiveness. I usually screenshot them and save them on my phone for quick and easy access when I need a good push. Below is my favorite from Dr. Heidi Green. She is a clinical psychologist and a self-empowerment guide who wrote a book called The Path to Self-Love and World Domination; another book that I highly recommend as a great read. In the book, when I came across a list called "things that can be true at the same time," I knew I had to save this list. It has helped me tremendously when struggling with forgiveness, and it's encouraged me to explore lengthening the list and finding other things that can be true at the same time.

Things That Can Be True at the Same Time

1. Your parents did the best they could, *and* their choices wounded you.
2. You love someone, *and* you know it's not healthy to keep them in your life.
3. You're terrified to take the next step, *and* you know it's the right thing to do.
4. You want to have healthy relationships, *and* unresolved trauma is making it difficult.
5. You're afraid to fail, *and* you believe in yourself.
6. You genuinely want to forgive someone, *and* you know it's not a good idea to keep them in your life. (I added this one.)

At the end of the day, no matter how you approach forgiveness and what method you find that works best for you, I just hope you find a way to do it and do it fast. Your life will become so much richer when you stop holding onto things that keep you locked inside a prison. Remember, it won't be an overnight fix, and most times, it won't be easy, but the risk and effort bring rewards that are totally beyond anything you could ever imagine.

Sandra has, oftentimes, been a guiding force in my life in dealing with forgiveness, even if she wasn't aware of it. She's taught me that no matter how difficult some things can be in life, many of those things can be solved with a big laugh because once you're able to laugh about it, you're moving in the right direction toward letting it go completely. Sandra, please forgive me for comparing us to a giraffe and a Tasmanian devil. Although, I have a hunch that you would agree with my description completely, and I'm sure very soon we will have a great big laugh about it.

Forgive everything and everyone. I've learned it's the key to a peaceful life and a calm heart.

10

A Fearless Legend

It doesn't matter who you used to be; what matters is who you
decide to be today. You are not your mistakes. You are not
your mishaps. You are not your past. You are not your
wounds. You can decide differently today and at every
moment. Remember that. You are offered a new opportunity
with each breath to think, choose, decide and act
differently in a way that supports you in being all that
you are capable of being. You are not less than.
You are enough.

—Brittany Josephina

I CAN RECALL my first, and what I hope is my last, experience with
kidney stones as if it just happened yesterday. If you've experienced
that before, then you know exactly what I'm talking about. If you
haven't, I attest that it is a pain unlike any other.

The night before all hell broke loose, I was getting ready for
bed and noticed a little discomfort in my lower left back. Because I
was also in the middle of a full renovation of my home, I chalked it
up to lifting something incorrectly and that I had no doubt pulled a
muscle. I took some ibuprofen and went to bed.

The next morning, although I'm grateful for it now, is not a
morning that I would ever wish on anyone. It's certainly not some-

thing I would choose to go through again in my life. The pain in my lower back was still there but considerably mild in comparison to what it evolved into. I made my coffee and sat down to start my morning ritual of reading, writing, and meditation. Midway through listening to my affirmations playlist on my phone and watching the sunrise over the mountain outside my window, a surge of excruciating pain rushed into my entire lower left abdomen. It was so intense that within moments, I vomited, then passed out. Fortunately, I was sitting on the couch, so I didn't fall and hit my head on anything. When I regained consciousness, I dialed 911.

A group of five paramedics arrived within minutes and began the process of hooking me up to various monitors, taking my vitals, and ultimately injecting a strong pain reliever into the IV line they had already started. I remember freaking out to the extreme because I'm the type of person that likes to have all the information, and in this case, nobody could explain what was going on inside my body. What I was physically experiencing paled in comparison to the scenarios that were playing out in my mind. Was I dying? I had no idea. All I knew is that I couldn't stand, sit, or lie down. No position made me comfortable, and the injected pain medication wasn't even slightly taking the edge off.

I'm grateful for the lead paramedic, and I can remember how compassionate and kind he was with me. He placed his hand on my shoulder and very firmly encouraged me to just breathe and find a way to calm down. He assured me that nothing life-threatening was happening, and this gave me some solace. They wheeled me out on a gurney to the waiting ambulance, and off to the emergency room we went. During transport to the hospital, the paramedic in the ambulance, a very kind young woman, gave me another injection of very strong pain medication, yet still, nothing was taking the pain away. By this point, my mind was going berserk. Maybe the first guy didn't know what he was talking about, and something much graver was happening to me. She assured me that we were almost at the hospital and that everything was going to be fine.

We arrived, and the emergency team immediately gave me the strongest pain medication they had on hand, and with that, all of the pain disappeared. Finally, I could really breathe and start to relax. A plethora of physical exams followed, and within an hour, the results came back telling us all that I had a large kidney stone that was on the verge of passing, but that I wasn't out of the woods in terms of pain and discomfort for the foreseeable future. Before this day, I had never been in an emergency situation and had never spent time in a hospital. All of the scans and blood tests were overwhelming for me, but at last, I was content with knowing that it was something, although painful, that would pass with no harm left to my body. I relaxed into the situation and eventually fell asleep.

A few hours later, the doctor returned to my room, reviewed the test results with me, prescribed some take-home medication to help me eventually pass the stone, and with that, sent me home to recover. The next couple of days continued with an extreme amount of pain and discomfort as the stone continued to move through my system, and during the night of the fourth day, it finally passed out of my body. Relief finally arrived.

Physical pain is one thing, and thankfully, most physical pain in life can be quickly addressed and corrected. Emotional pain, however, is a totally different ball game. For a large part of my life, and for whatever reasons (reasons I'm still investigating to this day), I seem to attract and allow the wrong people into my life. Those choices absolutely stemmed from not feeling valuable or valued in the relationship, and it's taken me years to get to a place where I started recognizing those bad choices a lot more quickly, yet I'm still thankful for all of the heartache and lessons that I've learned along the way because they have made me a much stronger and much more fearless person.

I met my friend Shannon during the latter part of 2008, and from the beginning, her maternal instinct was on point. To this day, she has been such an instrumental influence and guiding force that helped me identify certain patterns and beliefs I held that allowed me to continually suffer through so many one-sided friendships and relationships. We've spent many nights over the years, either in person or on the phone, with her trying to help me understand and see the people and situations I was choosing to let into my life, and I will be forever grateful for her friendship and tutelage surrounding this area of my life. I can imagine she must have thought many times, *Why can't he just get it and understand that he is causing all of this drama in his life?* That didn't deter her, however, from being the ever-present guide for me as I struggled to figure it out for myself.

After many therapy sessions with Shannon through the years, one day, it finally clicked. I was afraid: Afraid of not pleasing people. Afraid I wasn't good enough to have friends. Afraid people were only being my friend for what they could get from me. In terms of relationship, you name it, and I was probably afraid of it on some level.

Through the experience with my kidney stone and a multitude of conversations with Shannon, I can finally say I have learned a life lesson that I will keep with me for the rest of my life. I've been able to see the vast difference between danger and fear. Danger is something that is legitimately happening to you or around you, and fear is the dialogue we create in our minds. The latter isn't real at all; it's just a story and a false one at that. It's through that understanding that I've come to know and believe what being fearless really means and how, when I apply fearlessness to my life, I can truly lead the life I was destined to experience.

What is fear? Why does it have the ability to totally dismantle our thinking, our emotions, and our rationale? How can we be such logical people, yet our logic flies out the window in the face of fear? I set out to find the answers to these profound questions, and here is what I found.

Although there are many underlying elements of fear and triggers that engage our fear response, for the purpose of this chapter, I've chosen to highlight the three most common fear factors. In my opinion, these are the roots of all of the other possible manifestations of fear in our lives.

Fear Factor 1

Fear of failure. We have all failed at something in our lives, but I want to be very clear. Just because you have failed at a project, a relationship, or a dream, that doesn't mean that you are a failure. The reality is, you tried something, you trusted someone, you pursued something, and it didn't work out. Don't lose sight of that reality in these situations because that's how the fear creeps into your life more and establishes itself as part of your story. It's not real; it is only your perception. Start today, by shifting your perception. You tried something, you trusted someone, you pursued a dream, and it didn't work out that time; that doesn't mean it will never work out in your favor. Buying into the perception that it happened once means it will continue to happen allows fear to be a crippling presence in your life. You are constantly changing and evolving. If something didn't work out the first time, the beauty of life and an ever-changing landscape gives us all the opportunity to try again. You have two choices here: you can give in to the crippling perception that things will never work out, or you can choose to pick yourself up, dust yourself off, and go for it again. Each time you rise in the face of a failed project, a failed relationship, or a failed dream, not only do you become more self-confident, but you also diminish the power of fear more and more each time.

Fear Factor 2

Fear of uncertainty. The only constant in life is change. Knowing that also presents the realization that the only certainty in life is uncertainty. Why not embrace that? We have legitimate control over a few things in our life. We can control how we eat, sleep, and show up for our responsibilities. We also have full control over how we choose to dream and envision the experience of life. The remaining things in our life experience: other people, circumstances, and outcomes are not within our control. Because of this, we have the opportunity to embrace uncertainty. Creating certainty through uncertainty is a skill that you can absolutely harness and make a more ever-present part of your daily existence. We need both certainty and uncertainty to lead productive lives. Although uncertainty and change are always going to be a part of life, you still get to choose your reaction. You can let the uncertainty crash on top of you and debilitate your outlook, or you can choose to embrace it and be curious about the next things that are coming into your life. You get to choose.

Fear Factor 3

Fear of rejection. We've all experienced rejection on some level in our lives. Don't be fooled because you will experience rejection again; however, just because someone rejects you, it doesn't mean that you are unworthy in any way. All humans as creative and spiritual beings make decisions for their lives for all sorts of reasons. Unfortunately, we make decisions most of the time unconsciously and based usually on past conditioning in our lives. I have learned that when someone rejects you, it's best to respond with the utmost grace and compassion that you can. The person who rejected you is on their own journey through life. At the end of the day, don't let rejection from someone make you believe that you are, in any way, unworthy of the best things and the best people in your life. Accept the rejection and move forward, surrounding yourself with the people that truly want to experience life by your side.

Overall, fear is neither good nor bad. It is a natural human emotion that arises out of real or perceived danger. If the danger is very much real, our bodies are wonderful at triggering the fight or flight response. It is one of the greatest protection mechanisms that we possess. Anxiety, however, is fear that is based on a perceived threat that isn't reality. It most often, if not always, arises from fearing something in the future; something for which we actually have no control.

There is good news, however. We do have total and complete control over how we choose to react in the face of fear. Having faced fear myself, I've come up with some techniques that have helped me embrace it. I'm absolutely not perfect in this realm, but I've chosen to celebrate that I'm a constant work in progress, and I know that by continuing to implement the following techniques into my daily life, fear will become a much smaller force on my future.

Fearlessness Tip 1

Sit with the fear, get comfortable. We have so many exit strategies at our disposal for dealing with fear. Most often, we choose drugs, alcohol, smoking, sex, television, and the comfort of others in an effort to escape feeling the fear. I want to encourage you to just sit with the fear. Exist with it and, instead of letting your mind run rampant and control the narrative, analyze in those quiet moments how the fear makes you feel physically in your body. Notice the pain; fear bottled up doesn't go away, it only gets stronger. And when it continues to gain strength, it can manifest itself in so many harmful ways in your body and in your relationships. I've experienced firsthand that when I make the fear tangible and hold it in front of me like a physical object, I can see all of its hidden aspects. When I shine the light of actual reality and compassion on the fear, I've noticed how quickly it gets smaller and smaller until, ultimately, it dissipates.

Fearlessness Tip 2

Celebrate your goodness. One of my favorite ways to visualize and celebrate my goodness is in meditation. In those private and completely serene moments, I'm able to understand and accept that I have so much goodness inside of me. I come to know that I'm a part of every single moment. I get to feel that I am enough in every situation; this is an incredible confidence booster. No matter how you feel at any given time of the day, meditation has taught me that there is an abundant amount of goodness inside of me; this helps me deal with the fear of rejection, fear of being vulnerable, and the fear of being judged. In a meditative state, I've learned that fear cannot exist. There is so much love and light in that space that it prevents fear from even attempting to knock on the door.

Fearlessness Tip 3

Find joy in uncertainty. It's completely normal that we want to have a certain amount of certainty, permanence, and stability in our lives; however, life is filled with the opposite of those things, and I've come to appreciate the instability, shakiness, uncertainty, and chaos that life has to offer. When you are in the middle of that chaos or uncertainty, embrace it. You are being presented with an enormous opportunity to grow. When you experience moments of discomfort, wrap your arms around that experience and know that what is coming is far better than what has gone. Remind yourself constantly that you are an evolving being and that change is not your enemy. You can focus on the road ahead and not get stuck in the mud puddles of fear along the way. Whatever you do, don't become a prisoner to your thoughts because your mind will always present so many "what-if" scenarios if you allow it to. Find moments of peace to remind yourself that you're okay, you're going to be okay, and all will work out for the best in your life. Lastly, your mindset during uncertainty is absolutely everything. Give yourself regular pep talks to prevent going into a state of depression about the things that are changing around you. Fear can't exist in that mindful state.

The more opportunities I've had to talk with people who are experiencing any amount of struggle in their life, the more I see how fears are truly holding us back. Fear prevents us from constructing healthy and productive habits. Fear makes it all too easy for us to procrastinate. Fear blocks us from finding work that we are truly passionate about. Fear disables us from building true and lasting relationships and from connecting to our relationships at a much deeper level. Overall, fear keeps us from being completely happy in each moment of our day.

Conquering fear will not be an overnight event. In most cases, you won't completely conquer it in your lifetime, but you can learn to understand its place in your life and do everything you can to be prepared when it decides to show up at any given moment. For me, it's in the little things. It's having a vision. It's seeing and feeling with absolute emotion. It's being prepared and knowing what tools you have in your arsenal to combat the effects of fear. Be playful with it. Find reading materials or songs or podcasts that focus your mind on accepting the flow of change. Put it into daily practice and watch it grow.

You won't wake up tomorrow completely fearless. The biggest and most important lesson I've learned is that when you hold fear, whatever it may be, in the forefront of your conscious mind, it has no choice but to shrink until it disappears. I strongly encourage you to find the ways that work for you to lead a more fearless and, thereby, a more tranquil life.

11

A Compassionate Legend

We are all equal in the fact that we are all different. We
are the same in the fact that we will never be the same. We
are united by the reality that all colors and all cultures are
distinct and individual. We are harmonious in the reality
that we are held to this earth by the same gravity. We don't
share blood, but we share the air that keeps us alive.

—C. JoyBell C.

THE WORLD IS full of critics today. I've said it before, and I will say
it again. I can't make watching the news a regularly occurring habit.
If anything, I prefer to read the news that I want to be updated on
because, in reading, I find that criticism exists on a minimal level. On
the rare occasion that I do watch the news, it doesn't last long before
I shut the television off. Everyone is a critic. It's all bad news because
the news anchors, lately, only report the negative side of any given
situation or circumstance. Whether the topic is politics, pop culture,
health issues, or the environment, the doom and gloom reports just
flood the screen, and the barrage of fear and judgment overwhelm
me. That is not the person I want to be, so I choose to avoid the news
as much as possible.

Would you agree that the world needs more compassion?
Accepting and choosing to see life through someone else's eyes and

the gravity of their experience through life, without judgment, is a trait that can be and should be cultivated more often in our lives. The opportunity for compassion presents itself every single day. We either choose to choose it, or we choose to look the other way. It's a choice; no more and no less.

Let's face it together! We could all deal with a lot more compassion; compassion for all living things. This includes the living and breathing planet that we all inhabit.

There is an old Amish proverb that simplifies compassion for me, and I revisit this proverb time and time again. It says, "Instead of putting someone else in their place, put yourself in their place." I simply love this. It serves as a great reminder that everyone is experiencing life at the same time, and every life is unique in its own right. It reminds me that while we all may be taking the same exam called life, everyone has different test questions; therefore, everyone has different answers based on their individual experience of life. Realizing that, who are we to judge others? All answers are correct for the other person because their personal journey is dictating the responses to the exam. With that said, I want to encourage you to remember that no matter the answers to your test, stand strong in the knowledge that:

1. You're allowed to be a masterpiece *and* a work in progress *all at the same time.*
2. Following that logic, then so are all other people.

For me, that's the deeper meaning of compassion. Everyone can be taking their exam, and we can find a way to be okay with their answers because we don't get scored for their test results.

There was a great meme circling social media not long ago that I just fell in love with. It told the story of sunflowers. On a sunny day, sunflowers turn and face the sun to absorb its energy. On a cloudy day, sunflowers turn and face each other to share energy. Now, I did some research, and although those statements are not factually accurate, I still think it serves as a great life lesson when discussing compassion. Compassion is the realization that we all experience gray days, and the great reminder is to turn and face someone who is struggling and share your energy. You never know how it might change their day for the better.

My friend Marios is the epitome of living a compassionate life. He models this character trait on a daily basis, and it's one of the main things that attracted me to him. We met for the first time at an event in Europe during the summer of 2012. You could just feel his compassionate energy from the very first moment, and I was drawn to it. Since I know that the universe responds to your deepest intentions, I know that Marios came into my life at a time when I was looking for more ways to be compassionate. In any given situation, he has proven to be the first one to be open and the last one to form a judgment. For as long as I've known him, he's always been so skilled at seeing a person or situation from many sides and then moving forward into that circumstance with unconditional love.

Through the years of our incredible friendship, we've had many conversations surrounding the larger meaning of life, and the conversation most often centers around unconditional love, acceptance, and compassion for all people and all situations. After closely observing this character trait in him for years, and after a significant amount of research, I've been led to a place where I can clearly identify the awesome benefits of leading a more compassionate existence. One of the leading articles I found on *Psychology Today* written by Emma Seppälä PhD in November 2012 was particularly enlightening and led to even more research on my part. I'd like to share what I found with you.

Compassion Increases Your Happiness

It is truly better to give than to receive. Can you recall a time when you gave freely to someone else without expecting anything in return? Do you remember how that felt afterward? I stumbled across three very enlightening studies that proved the positive effects of giving to others in profound ways.

Study 1

A brain study conducted and led by Jordan Grafman who is a neuroscientist from the National Institute of Health definitively proved that the "pleasures centers" in the brain (i.e., the parts of our brains that light up when we experience types of pleasure [like dessert, money, or sex]), are equally active when we observe someone giving money to a charity as when we receive money ourselves!

Study 2

In this profound study led by Harvard Business School Professor Michale Norton that was eventually published in *Science Magazine*, participants were given a sum of money. Half of the participants were encouraged to spend the money on themselves, and the other half were encouraged to spend the money on others. When the study concluded, participants that spent money on others felt significantly more joyful than the people that had spent money on themselves; Therefore, it is suggested that giving to others increases our well-being to a greater degree than spending money on ourselves.

Study 3

This one is for the parents of small children out there! A recent experiment by Elizabeth Dunn and her team at the University of British Columbia showed that, even in children as young as two-years-old, giving things to others increased their happiness more than when they received things for themselves.

Compassion Grows Your Wisdom

Broadening our perspective beyond a place of self-focus reduces anxiety and depression. When we are anxious or depressed, we are literally just focusing on ourselves and the challenges we are facing. However, research and studies go a long way to prove that as soon as you shift your thinking and actions to a place where you are giving to others, the anxiety and depression become significantly diminished. Putting more compassion and giving to others into practice allows you to see more challenges that others face, which ultimately brings a lot of wisdom to your life, because now you know that you aren't the only one facing challenges in life. You are not alone.

Compassion Makes You More Attractive

Here, I'm not talking about the latest fads in wrinkle creams or the newest and best supplements to make our physiques more sculpted. There is nothing wrong with being healthy and looking the way you want if it makes you happy; however, if you are doing those things to mask your own fear of vulnerability in a relationship, then creams and supplements are not the answer. In fact, with relationships, studies show that both men and women revere kindness in others as one of the most sought-after traits in a friend or life partner. Of course, we all want love, solid relationships, and a strong social support system in our lives. With that said, no matter how much you spend on the latest in cosmetic advances, cultivating compassion in your life would be a far more effective and far less expensive option to building stronger relationships with people.

Compassion Attracts Abundance

Remember when we talked about the law of attraction? Let's revisit it here again. When we give things to others, whether that be time, money, or material possessions, we are operating from a place of abundance. The universe, because of this vibration, responds to you by giving you even more abundance. The cycle repeats over and over; this is a no-brainer for me. If I want more abundance in my life, then I must start with giving to others from a mindset of abundance.

Compassion Boosts Your Health

When you feel good, you do good. I was fascinated by the studies I stumbled on by Ed Diener and Martin Seligman. They found that when we connect with other people in meaningful ways, it can help us welcome better mental and physical health into our lives. They also discovered that it could speed up recovery from ailments and diseases. Furthermore, incredible research by Stephanie Brown at Stonybrook University has shown that it could even lengthen our lifespan.

That begs the question for me. How can giving more compassion improve our overall health? Steve Cole and Barbara Fredrickson have found a great answer to that question. They evaluated inflammation on a cellular level with people who described themselves as "very happy." You've probably read many times that inflammation is at the root of cancer and other diseases and that inflammation is higher in those who live with a lot of stress. That would mean that inflammation would be lower in people with higher levels of happiness, right? It's not so cut and dry apparently. They found this was only the case for certain "very happy" people. They discovered in their studies that people who were happy because they lived the "good life" (a life about keeping up appearances and retaining all of their good fortune just for themselves) had high inflammation levels, but that, in other cases, people who were happy because they lived a life of purpose and meaning (sharing their abundance with others) had low inflammation levels. A life centered around compassion, altruism, and purpose is obviously the lifestyle to adopt. It leads to a richer and more meaningful existence, and it breeds an abundance of true happiness in your life.

Giving to others is not going to break your bank account. Giving comes in many forms. It could be money if you have it to give, but

I've learned that giving other things like time, understanding, and a listening ear is far more valuable than the almighty dollar. Over the years, my friend Marios has given so many parts of himself on a regular basis, and it didn't cost him a dime. Whether he knows it or not, he has modeled a life of compassion for me. He spent nothing, but he gained so much in terms of a richer life filled with meaning and purpose; that's the life I want.

The great Maya Angelou said, "People will often forget what you said. People will often forget what you did. People will never forget how you made them feel." I couldn't agree more. I've used her wise words for many years in my personal and professional life, and I've seen firsthand the impact that approach has on the life of others and my life. Today, I strive to include a mindset of compassion in every single activity that I participate in. I've cultivated my own method to make it a daily practice. Hopefully, these tips will help you along on your journey of becoming a more compassionate person.

Compassion Concept 1

Compassion creates more caring. Earlier on in this book, I mentioned *The Eight Verses for Training the Mind.* I love all eight verses and use them daily to support a more positive mindset. Verse 4 stands out to me the most, though, in relation to offering more compassion. It says, "When I see ill-natured people, overwhelmed by wrong deeds and pain, may I cherish them as something rare, as though I had found a treasure trove." We encounter people on a daily basis that are in some level of pain and suffering; this could be physical pain, which is easy to spot, or it could be deep-seated emotional pain, which is not so easy to see. Regardless, when you can observe that someone is in pain, find a way to offer them compassion and caring, even if that offering is in silence. By doing this, you will circumvent the habit of rushing in to be the judge of their behavior. It's been said many times that people are going through something that you know nothing about, so just be kind in all encounters that you have.

Compassion Concept 2

Compassion changes consciousness. Try it today. Try showing compassion to someone who has harmed you and pay attention to the outcome, but more importantly, pay attention to how you feel afterward. Even if they don't respond positively in the moment, trust that you have planted a seed that now has the chance to bloom. But remember, you're the planter, you are not the gardener of their life; they still have a choice to make. They can receive your compassion and let it grow, or they can turn a blind eye. Nonetheless, your only responsibility is to be the planter of kindness and compassion. Whatever they decide to do with your offering is literally none of your business. You've given a gift, and your only responsibility afterward is to monitor how giving compassion grows you forward so that you can continue to give it freely to other people. The idea here is that the more people who freely spread compassion on a more regular basis, it will begin to spread across the planet in profound ways.

Compassion Concept 3

Compassion curtails craziness. There is no point in wasting your peace trying to figure out why something happened the way it did or why a person is acting the way they are. Offering compassion in those moments will prevent a lot of frustration and anger in you. We will never benefit by allowing mixed emotions to grow inside of us. When they do fester inside of you, it can have a direct link to how you treat everyone else in your life.

Compassion Concept 4

Compassion combats cynicism. When we see something, we don't like or understand, natural human behavior is to become the critic. Being the critic is the easy way out. Don't become that cynic; it's not worth it. It requires very little effort. It takes a lot more mindfulness and discipline to realize and accept that everyone is on their individual journey through life, and their choices or behavior are based on that experience. Meet people where they are, not where you wish they were. Simply find a way to view their behavior as a very rare gift, a treasure trove because we can find so much value and lessons in simply observing, sending compassion, and moving on.

Compassion Concept 5

Compassion crosses caverns. When you offer compassion, most people will likely be caught off guard. We've become numb to it because compassion doesn't have a strong enough presence in our world today. They are used to being on the other side of the cliff, on edge with everyone being a critic, so you have an opportunity to surprise them and take them off the edge. Cross the cavern and offer compassion and see what happens in your life and, hopefully, be able to see the change that will one day take place in theirs.

Compassion Concept 6

Compassion ceases cruelty. We witness a lot of cruelty in today's society: cruelty to each other, cruelty to animals, cruelty to the environment. What we need is much more compassion. Compassion has the innate ability to solve many of the challenges we experience as the collective human race. Start by using it to end cruelty in and around your life and let that expand to more and more people. Implementing compassion into your daily life with the hope that it will continue to spread is each of our individual responsibility.

My deepest hope for this world is that we will all find a way to spread compassion to everyone that we meet. Compassion is the truest answer to most of our worldly and personal life challenges because it is steeped in unconditional love and acceptance of all things.

We are all connected—our gifts, our time, our hope and dreams. Although we may lead independent lives, that doesn't mean that we are separate from one another. We all bleed the same and breathe the same, and hopefully, when a compassion revolution comes to this planet, we can finally all begin to heal the same.

Be more compassionate starting today my friends.

12

A Present Legend

Most people never heal, because they stay in their heads, replaying corrupted scenarios. Let it go.

—S. McNutt

I GREW UP believing so many things about myself that ended up not being true. My father passed away when I was only seven years old, so for the remainder of my youth, my mother did the absolute best she could as a single parent. She taught me and my brother the best based on what she knew, whether they were good lessons or not-so-good ones at the end of the day. She did the best with what she had, and I will always love my mother for accepting the challenge of raising two boys alone. In my opinion, she didn't always get it right, but none of us get it right all the time. For me, she still gave birth to me, giving me the opportunity to experience this wonderful thing called life, and that deserves the utmost respect and reverence.

After the shock of my dad's death wore off, we continued forward in our little family unit and did the best we could. In my formative years that followed, I remember feeling unimportant, unheard, and for the most part, feeling like an alien in my own family. My brother got the majority of the attention, mainly because he was the one always getting into trouble. In my mind, I was the second child who did everything I could to please my mom in the hopes that I would be making her life a little easier. I always got good grades in school. I was dutiful during my piano lessons. I tried my best to be the high achiever in sports because I felt that was the expectation, although I was never really good at sports nor did I enjoy them.

One of the most painful memories from my childhood was being at a family reunion one summer and hearing the N-word for the first time. I use "N-word" because I won't even give power to saying the full word and giving credence to just how derogatory and vicious that word is. I remember when I heard it, I quickly understood they were using it to describe someone with a darker skin tone. Even at that young age, I knew the word was inflammatory, based on hate, and I instantly vowed it was a word I would never use.

I won't call my family racist and close-minded because, although true, it wouldn't be a very kind statement. What I will say is that a large majority of my family unit demonstrated extreme racism, bigotry, and a sheer lack of desire in understanding any people that weren't exactly like them. For me, growing up, that meant if you weren't White, Southern, Christian, and straight, then you were living a life of sin, and you had no real value on this earth.

We were a family that went to church every Sunday and Wednesday night professing our love for our faith and love for all mankind, so it was always odd and uncomfortable for me that we were also the same family every other day of the week that would not waste a moment putting others down, pouring on judgment of others whenever the opportunity presented itself, and not doing much of anything that resembled the teachings of Christianity that we claimed to love so much. This was always weird for me; I just didn't know why. I thought I was totally weird. I instinctually knew somewhere deep inside that I didn't agree with any of it, but that was the only landscape I had ever been shown; there had to be more.

It wasn't until I moved away in my mid-twenties that I started to gain clarity on the stark contrast between what I was taught growing up and what I actually believe about myself and other human beings. Unlearning those early life lessons is something that I still have to work at every day, but it has been an amazingly liberating process. The best tool I've come to rely on to deprogram my mind from those childhood lessons and prepare for the life I want to lead is the power of being present.

Presence: It's not the past. It's not the future. It's right now! Once you gain an understanding of the things that usually prevent you from existing in the present moment, you then have the ability to navigate around them and truly exist in the only moment we all are guaranteed to have—this moment right now.

For me, there are two main culprits that keep us out of the present moment: the mind and outside influences. Your mind presents you with emotions like worry, uncertainty, and fear. You also, at any given moment, can have a racing mind or a wandering mind; none of these are living in the present moment. While it can be difficult at first to live in the present moment, there is so much published proof about how practicing present moment mindfulness on a regular basis can increase your quality of life in so many wonderful ways. Let's take a look at those benefits.

Better Health

Simply choosing to exist in the present moment and that moment only from day to day has a direct impact on your physiological and psychological health. The reduction of stress and anxiety in your life will show immediate benefits such as lowering your blood pressure, preventing diseases of the heart, and combatting obesity. From a psychological standpoint, people who incorporate mindfulness into their daily routine have been shown to exhibit much higher levels of self-worth and emotional well-being.

Improvement in All Your Relationships

You probably have that friend or a few friends that every time you're out to dinner together, they spend the majority of their time on the phone, usually scrolling through social media or taking selfies, in an attempt to capture their perfectly posed moment from the evening that they can later share with all of their followers. How annoying is that?

With my friends, we have a simple rule. When we are together, we choose to be in that moment and enjoy everything the moment has to offer. We put our phones away and just enjoy each other's company. Being with people, who, although, physically present, but are otherwise unavailable is frustrating and, therefore, attempting to build or strengthen your relationship with them proves to be a challenge. On the other hand, do you remember what it feels like to be with a person who is fully existing with you in the present moment? How much richer has that experience and relationship been? For me, it's much more enjoyable because we are making a truer and deeper connection. Also, for other people, it allows them to connect with you more authentically when you are fully present during times of connection.

Increased Self-Control

When you develop the practice of having greater control over your mind, body, and emotions, you lead a much calmer life because you aren't held captive to a wandering mind or a mind that races out of control. When you become the observer of your thoughts rather than falling captive to the thoughts themselves, you tend to lead a much healthier and happier life. Try it next time when you feel overwhelmed by a thought. Sit with it and, instead of being the thought, shift your mind consciously to being the observer of the thought. Doing this has helped me tremendously in navigating a lot of the unconscious negative self-talk that stalks our minds from time to time.

Your presence is a complete gift; a gift to you and a gift to others. I know we often think of gifts as something wrapped up with a great big bow on top. If I can make a leap right here, those are presents. We are talking about *presence*. When put into practice, it breeds more meaningful connections, improves your overall well-being, and keeps you from reliving the past or projecting into the future; two things you cannot control. The power of living in the present moment is the gift that keeps on giving; it shows love, support, and kindness to yourself and to others.

My favorite moment of complete presence is making my first cup of coffee or tea in the morning. I actively engage with listening to the sound of the grinder grinding the beans then feeling the pressure in my hands as I tamp down the ground beans. I continue my present moment awareness by enjoying the aroma as the espresso drips into my cup and then listening to the whirring sound of the steam wand as it aerates my oat milk. I find more appreciation and definite humor as well when I start pouring the steamed milk into the espresso and trying to do latte art, which I'm confident that I will never possess the skill to do like the trained baristas do. I like this moment of presence because it's right after I wake up. It sets the tone and reminds me to be present in more activities throughout my day.

You can give the gift of your presence to so many things throughout your day. Your exercise: Listening to the rise and fall of your breath. Meditation—pushing out the thoughts that want to intrude and being present with the silence. Diving into a project at work and giving it your full attention without distraction.

It's, no doubt, going to require patience as you put more attention on living in the present moment. I love what Mark Nepo says about this. He says, "For the flower, it is fully open at each stage of its blossoming. We do ourselves a great disservice by judging where we are in comparison to some final destination. This is one of the pains of aspiring to become something. The stage of development we are in is always seen against the imagined landscape of what we are striving for. So where we are—though closer all the time—is never quite enough." I couldn't agree with this statement more, and I am guilty of not being the most patient person when striving to be more present.

But from Mark's beautiful words, I have now found a much greater appreciation for how spending time in nature can actually keep me in the present moment for such a long time.

Observe how a seed grows into a flower. It undergoes many transformations, and each stage leads to the next. At times, it seems the plant has stopped growing, but really, it's resting and gathering energy for the next phase. Some phases require more energy than others, and the plant rests longer in preparation. This is the song of creation, just like in a musical composition, the rests are equally as important as the notes, and without both, the song could not exist. There is beauty in every nuance of the plant's gradually changing form, and we are the same.

In the great garden of life, we each grow at our own pace. Paying attention to the state you are in presently is nourishing. It can tap into a deeper vitality, which can provide long-lasting stability and support; this can ease frustration and impatience, which often comes from feeling lack. Filling that space with curiosity, wonder, and appreciation can bring contentment. Out of that contentment can emerge a knowing that yes, this right now, this present moment is absolutely enough.

The plant kingdom has been living and evolving far longer than humans. In fact, plants possess ancient wisdom and are powerful allies for our journey through life. They can help us to align with the rhythm of the days, the seasons, and the innate timing of our journey. Communing with plants can shift us from negative emotional states to a grounded and calm presence, a sense of wholeness. This is why I like hiking so much; it puts me smack-dab in the middle of the present moment where there is no visible way out, and I just love that!

Impatience is cheap and easy; it's natural conditioning that can and should be broken. When you absolutely can't control something, relish in the patience and the knowing that you are flowering into the exact flower you are supposed to be.

It's scientifically proven that impatience has all sorts of physiological effects that we don't need. It raises your blood pressure. It releases adrenaline. Knowing this, I encourage you to ask yourself these questions: Do I want to be in a state of fight or flight? Or do I want to be in a state of rest, healing, and repair? The choice is yours, so strive to choose patience and to exist in the present moment more often. Just accept the part of the journey you are on. Please don't fall into the temptation to try and control things or skip very valuable stages of your flowering. Cultivate a mindset of tolerance, for example, by saying to yourself, "I'm just going to accept this part of my journey and my growth. This moment is relevant and vital, and I'm going to enjoy it for all it's worth."

Why do we struggle to live in the present moment, and what can we do about it? As with anything, existing in the present moment is going to require forethought and application on a regular basis. It's just like learning a new game or activity. Practice makes perfect, remember that. We are all so conditioned to be on autopilot most of the time. We act and think out of habit and past conditioning. We form thoughts and judgments without conscious awareness. We just react. We spend most of our energy rehashing the past or rehearsing the future: wishing, hoping, planning, ruminating, missing, regretting.

We are disconnected from what is happening in our lives—right now, in the present moment—and even within our own bodies and minds. In this mode, emotions seem to just sort of happen to us, and we might not acknowledge them, understand them, or realize we can control them, or we might try to dodge emotions or shut them out. Either way, this is a recipe for emotion to overwhelm us. When we are not in the moment, we don't actually feel our feelings, and that creates more of the very emotions we may wish to avoid. It also doesn't (and can't) solve the problems we are trying to escape.

Eight of the most common barriers that keep you from being mindful are:

1. thinking about the past and the future, this takes you out of the present moment;
2. multitasking;
3. being in denial;
4. attachment to thoughts or observations;
5. pushing away thoughts or observations;
6. having unclear intentions;
7. having a lack of compassion; and
8. judging, evaluating, analyzing, or criticizing.

There is light at the end of the tunnel, though. We can make another choice. We can switch off the autopilot and take the wheel ourselves. This starts with mindfulness. Anyone can do it, even those whose usual approach is a far cry from being mindful. Mindfulness is a skill like any other, so it can be learned. Also, like any other skill, the more you practice it, the better you will get at it, so here's my strongest recommendation on how to practice mindfulness: *pay attention*. And I mean, really pay attention: to things as they are, in the present moment, and that's it.

Now that you know that you should be paying more attention to the present moment, I would like to share with you a few of the things that I've implemented that help keep me in the present moment more often.

Presence Protocol 1

Power down your devices. We most definitely now live in the digital and virtual age. Technology has advanced to such an exponential degree, and it is embedded in so many of our daily tasks. Technology and the advances in social media are great for growing your business and keeping you connected with loved ones from afar, but the one thing technology will never be able to do is replace authentic human interaction. When it comes to your smart devices and being in the present moment, I have some advice: *put them away!* You can't be in two places at one time; this includes your smartwatch these days. By doing both, you're attempting to multitask and focus on two things at once, which your human brain is not designed to do. Putting away the device shows respect to the other person and shows them that you're truly engaged in what they have to say. Put them away in Zoom meetings, one-on-one conversations, face-to-face encounters, and watch your relationships expand.

Presence Protocol 2

Listen but don't think. We would all benefit greatly from the wise words of Thich Nhat Hanh when he said, "Compassionate listening is crucial. We listen with the willingness to relieve the suffering of the other person, not to judge or argue. We listen with all our attention." Unfortunately, most times, we aren't actively listening. People truly want to know that you hear them and see them, and we are all falling short of giving them that respect. I know because I've fallen into this trap myself. I've listened to my friends talk while wondering about completely random, inconsequential things, like when the next season of my favorite series will start up again or whether I made the best decoration decision in my bedroom. On my worst days, I've held a full conversation with someone while rehashing painful memories in my head or worrying about the many things I can't control. At the same time, many of us are conditioned to listen to respond, instead of listening just to gain understanding; this means you're thinking and not truly listening. You're only getting bits and pieces of what they are saying; this leads to misunderstandings and impatience.

Their talking is, no doubt, going to trigger your thoughts, memories, opinions, ideas you want to share, etc. Don't get lost in that. Regain focus and bring your attention back to what they are actually saying. It's human nature to sometimes do these things, but there's no denying it can make a huge difference for the people we love when we're fully present with them and actively listening.

Presence Protocol 3

Don't invite your ego to the party. If allowed to go unchecked, your own ego will hijack your thoughts every single time; this causes you to get swept up in your own self-centeredness and shuts off active listening.

It can also cause you to interrupt with your own stance or a counterargument. Practice being more mindful that the thoughts are there rather than focusing on the thoughts themselves and, in doing so, give your full nonjudgmental attention to the task or conversation at hand.

Presence Protocol 4

Take care of yourself first. This may seem odd to be first, but if your needs aren't met and you aren't full, how will you give something to someone else from an empty tank? If you're drained, it can cause you to be short and impatient with people when they are trying to connect with you. To make sure you are full, spend time doing things you are passionate about because that will keep you right smack-dab in the middle of the present moment. Perfecting your passions then teaching them to someone who wants to learn them is a great suggestion to build stronger connections with others and keep you both in the present moment.

Presence Protocol 5

Be proud of your proficiency. Practicing present moment awareness takes practice. Don't judge the rate at which you are moving forward. Don't base your progress on others. Celebrate that you are moving in the right direction at exactly the right pace *for you*! Don't rush yourself. Don't set unrealistic expectations for yourself. Promise yourself daily that you will move forward with a speed that is comfortable for you, and you won't judge the rate at which you are moving.

Judgment is one of the most common activities that keep you from being mindful and living in the present moment more often. Whether you are judging your experience as good, bad, or ugly, it's an obstacle to being fully present in the moment, and you do it all the time; everyone does. The way to do it less—the way to not let judging interfere with your ability to be mindful—is to increase your awareness of when you are judging and then simply stop judging.

Practicing presence, no doubt, builds better relationships. People respect and trust you more. Practicing presence in your own life builds your self-confidence and opens your awareness to so many more beautiful things around you that otherwise go completely unnoticed.

All we can really do in these human moments is be aware, accept ourselves as we are, and give ourselves permission to be perfectly imperfect. The best way to get present again is to accept that we sometimes won't be, let go when we struggle, and then try again.

13

A Free Legend

For a seed to achieve its greatest expression, it must come
completely undone. The shell cracks, its insides come out,
and everything changes. To someone who doesn't understand
growth, it would look like complete destruction.

—Cynthia Occelli

FAIR WARNING! THIS chapter, the last chapter, metaphorically speaking, is bound to be a powder keg. It's absolutely meant to be provocative. It most definitely won't be a chapter about one of my amazing friends and how they helped shape my life.

As we come to the close of this book, my full intention in writing this is to give all of us the opportunity to wake up and see what is happening all around, for the purpose of sparking true change within ourselves and true change throughout the world.

For most of my life, I've been a person that finds great comfort in music and, most importantly, the lyrics written and performed by musicians that I admire. Music and its lyrics have always managed to help me navigate many difficult times in my life. I believe music, for me, has a direct connection to my soul, and often, it opens up the ears of my soul, allowing me to deeply examine what I want the course of my life to be. I think that is the case for most of us in the world. One of my favorite performers in a recent song said in lyrics that still make me sit up and pay attention:

> *Freedom*
> *Freedom*
> *I can't move*
> *Freedom, cut me loose*
> *Singin', freedom*
> *Freedom*
> *Where are you?*
> *'Cause I need freedom, too*
> *I break chains all by myself*
> *Won't let my freedom rot in hell*
> *Hey! I'ma keep running*
> *'Cause a winner don't quit on themselves*

What are we doing! Are we free? And when I say "we," I mean all of us as the collective human race. I'm going to attempt, to the best of my ability, to outline the major concerns that I see are shaping our current and future experience of life. I apologize in advance if any of the language and opinions in this chapter are too strong, and I sincerely hope it doesn't make you angry. With that said, I'm completely okay if this chapter makes you incredibly uncomfortable because, at the core of my being, I do believe dynamic discomfort leads to dynamic change.

Let's start with how we nourish ourselves on a daily basis. Approximately 2,500 years ago, the father of modern medicine Hippocrates said, "Let food be thy medicine, and medicine be thy food." His intention was to educate and guide the human race with the knowledge that being extremely conscious of what we put into our bodies is the guaranteed way to enhance our physical experience during our life. However, today, we couldn't be further off track from that wise instruction. We eat food that makes us sick. Then, in search of a remedy, we take medicine that is, in my opinion, designed to keep us sick. We seek out the advice of medical professionals who are being directly compensated with loads of money to recommend the latest and greatest pharmaceutical that should ease our pain and suffering or, at the very least, mask our symptoms. What they don't tell us is, often, that very same remedy can create a slew of additional physiological challenges. Whether you agree or not, don't you find it even just a little strange that we've strayed so far from the wise words of Hippocrates into a place where, today, the medical profession barely acknowledges the importance of diet, much less are they willing to recommend a healthy diet as a solution to most medical problems. Instead, they choose to major in the prescription and distribution of high-powered drugs that have a singular focus—to right the wrongs of decades of body mismanagement. Now, I'm not at all saying that all doctors have gotten off course in their professions. What I'm actually wondering is when did the collective medical profession abandon its most sacred promise to "first do no harm"?

Sadly, we've also found a way to capitalize on and monetize pain and suffering. You see it all around. Look at celebrities and public figures as just one example. We cheer for the underdog on one hand until someone decides they are wrong, and then we collectively mount an offensive and defensive to target them, attack them, and break down every facet of their life publicly for our own entertainment; however, they are still just people like you and me. How would we feel if we had to wake up every day and read the world's opinions on our own lives? Just stop doing it, please. It's, in no way, productive and on a deeper level; it just highlights and focuses our attention on the imperfect nature of us all. My friends, we aren't designed to be perfect. We are designed to experience life, love others, and give compassion and encouragement to all of our fellow living creatures.

For the longest time, I was excited to watch the RBG (Ruth Bader Ginsberg) documentary on Netflix. I kept putting it off due to a busy schedule and, before you know it, sadly, she passed away. So after watching the news about her passing and seeing the details of her extraordinary life, I went to Netflix one evening to search for it, only to find that it had been removed, and now, I could only watch it if I was willing to pay for it. When and why did we decide that it was a great idea to capitalize on such an important life event like death?

Moving on, we've become addicted to social media, and even though all of the various platforms for connection and social interaction have—in such a profound manner—incubated a breed of narcissism never witnessed before in the history of humankind, we all still dial them up on a regular basis. For what purpose? Why are we so interested in a snapshot of a moment that has already happened? What's our connection to a moment from the past that has, most likely, been filtered? Do we really believe that a past moment should be the basis on which we construct our present moment and the model for how we will design and plan our future?

Social media can be a powerful tool for growing your business, no doubt. Used with mindful intentions it can provide a great connection point between colleagues, customers, and friends and serve as a great platform for sharing ideas and information. But, let's be honest, that's not how it's being used these days. It's used as a way to spy on other people and judge their choices in life. It's used to build people up and celebrate their achievements, only to later tear them down, eviscerate them, and publicly shame the person they are striving to be. Most recently, it's used to drive political agendas, vomit propaganda onto all of us, and strive to shape the way we see the world. You've all seen it. Why do we find value in doing that? How does it honor and elevate the experience of your life?

The social media companies monitor everything we look at online, and guess what, they purposefully then market to each of us individually based on what we are paying the most attention to online. Can't you see what's happening? Are you aware? I encourage you to pay attention the next time you are blindly scrolling through social media. Pay attention to the ads that are being presented to you on a regular basis; they are a direct reflection of how you view yourself in an online world. So the key is, if you don't like what you see, then change the way you see the world.

What else is happening? Daily, I'm confounded by the idea that a majority of the collective human species have become so racially, ethically, and morally indignant. A vast majority of people living with privilege because of their race or financial status continue to view the world while wearing blinders. They can't or don't want to see the plethora of injustices that are being inflicted on so many people because of their race, sexuality, gender, and social-economic status. We seem to knowingly or unknowingly agree to the terms of the "rich get richer and the poor get poorer" as well as "white is right and all other races don't matter." This mindset must change, and it must be now. We are all connected, and if we continue to travel in this direction where we devalue so many things in so many people, it's all of us, and I do mean *all*, that will ultimately pay the price.

Simply stated, Black Lives Matter shouldn't be a movement; rather, it shouldn't have to be a movement ever. How did we get to a place where we systemically believe that any race is less significant than another? Whether you look at the situations involving the killing by police of unarmed Michael Brown, George Floyd, Breonna Taylor, and Eric Garner in recent years or travel back to killings perpetrated by White supremacists on Medgar Evers, Emmitt Till, and Martin Luther King Jr. to name only a few during the Civil Rights Movement, it's all the same. The circumstances may change, only slightly, from incident to incident, but the infectious ignorance and hatred are identical.

I never could have imagined that we would be experiencing this type of chronic and seemingly incurable infection in today's society. I call it chronic because it's ever present and often lurking just beneath the surface. And like an infection, that often and without warning, rears its ugly head leading to great pain and suffering. So this chronic infection that was prevalent so many times throughout human history has now come back to visit us, and it's come back with a vengeance. There are many that believed after the end of the civil rights movement that we had solved the problem.

The same goes for the #MeToo movement in recent history. The symptoms are different, but the root of the infection is the same: greed, ego, and megalomania. The idea that some people, predominantly males, in powerful positions view others simply as property that they are entitled to possess whenever and wherever they choose is truly disturbing. Much like racial inequality that continues to surface, the #MeToo movement is the resurfacing of the chronic infection that has surrounded gender equality for centuries. But much like a dental abscess that requires the complete removal of the root in your tooth; we haven't gotten to the real root of racial injustice and gender inequality, and sadly, we are still quite a long way off from finding the cure, but the cure does exist.

The idea of a cure that is freely available relates to our planet as well. The desire for more convenience and items to be more readily available at the click of a button has created a downward spiral in which our planet is dying. You can turn away and refuse to accept that as fact, but it won't stop it from being true. Take a close look at the significant changes in climate that we are all experiencing; it's undeniable. We pollute the oceans daily, we poison our livestock with antibiotics and many other chemicals, only to turn around and wonder why our food makes us sick. We kill beautiful creatures for sheer sport, rather than out of necessity to feed our families. We annihilate large portions of our forests and, in some very sad cases, eliminate entire ecosystems. How long do we plan to survive and thrive on a planet that we have gone out of our way to suffocate?

There are many that would lazily question: This doesn't affect me, so why should I care, and even if I did care, what can I do to change it? The age-old argument that "it's just the way it's always been" or "it is what it is" should seriously be condemned, and a radical change in mindset be brought to the forefront in all of our lives. For me, it's a simple and very personal acknowledgment of my own individual accountability that will affect the collective good for all living things. Here's a profound truth that may help shape your thinking around this. Accountability feels like an attack when you're not ready to acknowledge how your behavior harms others.

Everything that we are all experiencing right now surrounding discrimination of any kind, racial injustice, gender inequality, persecution based on sexual orientation, depleting our world's natural resources, human trafficking, you name it because the list is so long, they are all connected. They are all a part of the same generational curse. The curse is formed out of our idea that "my needs are the most important thing no matter how they affect all other living things on this planet." I follow The Mind's Journal on Instagram, and one of my favorite postings that they made and that has helped me stay mindful of my personal responsibility to the greater good for all life says, "It's up to us to break generational curses. When they say, 'It runs in the family,' you tell them, 'This is where it runs out!'" It's up to all of us to stand up and say *no* to things that don't benefit all life on this planet.

There is hope, though, but it involves all of us deciding to move in the same direction of change. I love Cynthia Occelli's quote at the opening of this chapter because, yes, we must all become "*completely undone*" and see a radical change through to fruition. And trust me, I get it. Change is so very uncomfortable. Even though we can all agree that change is the only constant in our existence, agreeing doesn't make the application and execution of that agreement any less painful. It's painful because change brings up huge amounts of uncertainty for us, and that's okay. It's completely normal. Uncertainty is never going to be a welcome emotion, but I've learned that through acceptance of that uncertainty, I can spark change in my own life that will hopefully lead to the greater good for everyone and everything. Through tried-and-true experience, along with a lot of practice, I have developed for myself a solid approach to creating certainty in uncertain times.

What causes uncertainty for us? Simple, any form of change. We are used to being comfortable because with comfortability comes the idea that we are better equipped to predict the outcome of our lives; however, change is the only thing that will not change for us. It's a constant part of the cycle of life and our experience as living breathing beings. You still have a choice though. You can choose to ride the wave of change, or you can choose to let it crash upon you as you struggle to stay afloat.

Trust me, I get it. Change usually comes as a total surprise. You weren't at all prepared for what just happened. Everything in your life was going just perfect and then, *wham*! You get hit. It's frustrating because it feels like the universe is conspiring to sabotage your hopes, dreams, and goals that you have for your life. Our initial reaction in most cases is a very visceral one. But I urge you, *don't take it personally*. The key is to find ways to create certainty for your life while at the same time accepting that you can't control most things in life.

There is a great paradox at work, and it is: you need both certainty and uncertainty to live the most fulfilled and rewarding life. We need both forces to lead fulfilled, passionate, successful lives. The biggest issue that most people struggle with when it comes to change is dealing with uncertainty. Because there is no certainty about what will happen during a time of change, many people either try to control events or other people or they simply shut down. However, we know the emotion of uncertainty can unlock surprise and fun in our lives and can allow us to experience brand-new feelings, thoughts, beliefs, and strategies. Uncertainty can both paralyze and liberate, but you get to decide. We've all experienced uncertainty and will continue to have it as a part of our daily lives. A quote by Vincent Van Gogh—one of my favorites on this topic—says it best. He said, "For my part, I know nothing about certainty, but the sight of the stars makes me dream." So the secret to handling uncertainty is to just do everything you can to focus on progress, dream big, and create certainty where you can.

Creating certainty can help you adjust to a new city, to the loss of a loved one, to having to adjust to a new set of rules in life or in a relationship, or to the loss of a dream or something and someone you really wanted. You name it, that's all certainty is—an emotion that allows us to accomplish something that otherwise seems impossible. Let me show you how I've applied and put into practice a few things that have helped me tremendously in dealing with things I can't control so that I can be completely free.

Step 1: Create a Vision

Visualization is a very valuable tool. If you're unemployed, visualize your dream job.

If you've moved to a new city, visualize what you want your life to look like there. If you and your partner are having trouble, visualize your dream relationship and move in that direction. If you've lost a loved one, visualize and remember all of the things they brought to your life. If you're in a situation that seems impossible, and you aren't sure what to do, visualize the options that would make you the happiest and then just move forward in that direction.

Step 2: Make Your Resolution

Now, this is not like a New Year's resolution that often disappears as quickly as you made it. Make a real resolution. A resolution is a declaration of what you intend to do with your life. Then, cut off any other possibility. If this is what you truly want, then as they say, "Burn the boats." Don't develop plans B, C, and D in an attempt to flee your resolution. Make the plan and draw the roadmap that will get you to your destination. In doing all of this, don't forget: you can't control all events, but you can at least have certainty that you have a plan, and that realization has been very comforting for me.

Step 3: Find the Intention

Keeping your purpose and true intention for your new goal front and center at all times is crucial because without it, we tend to lose our emotional drive to do something. Make sure your reasons resonate deeply and, when possible, make sure you identify how they can help other people. These are not just superficial wants and desires. And remember, when you feel stuck, intentions come first, and answers come second. Don't get those mixed up.

Step 4: Make It a Part of Every Day

There's a part of your brain called the RAS—Reticular Activating System. Science has proven that this part of your brain determines what you notice in the world. So when you set a goal and focus on it every day and have strong enough reasons behind your intention, you trigger the RAS. Your brain then becomes so acute at noticing anything that comes into your world that could help you move forward in pursuit of your goals, and then, you guessed it, uncertainty vanishes once again because you are being presented with solutions that move you closer and closer to the life you want.

Step 5: Raise Your Standards

If you truly want real change, you have to raise your standards. Take a look at the parts of your life where you have a limitation and ask yourself when and why you decided to accept this. Most limitations are totally self-imposed and prevent us from making progress. Somehow, we've convinced ourselves that we only deserve the status quo, but *we deserve so much more!* You have to let go of limiting beliefs, limiting people, and start seeing each challenge as an opportunity to rise higher. This, of course, doesn't happen overnight, but the more you adopt these practices, thoughts, and behaviors, the more powerful your brain becomes at finding ways to bring you there.

Step 6: Adopt Rituals

You have to back up your newly raised standards with what makes those standards real—rituals. Rituals are something you do every day to build up momentum, and it becomes a clear path to your vision. You can totally demolish uncertainty with rituals. Condition your mind and body with a few small rituals to start: going for a short run, making a healthy breakfast, incorporating mantras into your day, catching up with a good friend every week, and doing something kind for yourself once a day, all the while having the certainty that you are making the world a much better place for you and everyone. Rituals are where the power lies; they define us. They help us put our newly raised standards into action. They help us deal with the uncertainty that comes with change. Remember, when uncertainty happens, we have the choice to relinquish control and shut down or to act. The choice is always yours.

Creating certainty like creating true change in yourself and in the world is not an overnight event: It's in the little things. It's in having a vision. It's in seeing and feeling with absolute emotion. It's in caring for other people. It's in calling to say "I love you" for no reason. It's in taking every opportunity to connect. It's in being playful with yourself, others, and life as a whole.

Change, no matter how devastating, does not have to define your life. You get to make that decision, and I know from firsthand experience that if you apply these steps to your life, no matter how lost you may feel at first, you will be able to start designing the life you want and living the life you deserve. My hope is that more and more of us around the world would realize the power we all have and start using that power to change ourselves and the world for the better.

We've all most likely heard the expression "The definition of insanity is doing the same thing over and over in the same manner but expecting a different result." Is that why life feels so insane so often today? We, most especially our leaders, are perfectly illustrating the insanity that we are all experiencing. I, for one, have chosen not to follow suit with them any longer. I want to be different. I want the world to be different. I want everyone to experience life on earth with a new moral code. A code that celebrates the individual. A code that condemns the offense yet still loves and finds compassion for the offender. A code that provokes all of us to value the life of every living thing. A code that supports the notion that all things are created equal and that true equality on every level is the only key to a happy, loving, and prosperous future together.

I close out this chapter with the most heartfelt encouragement to find your path to becoming a free legend in life. You deserve it. One person's freedom is a great encouragement for others in their life to become free as well. I leave you now with a few of the most encouraging words I've ever read from the late Maya Angelou on the topic of freedom:

I Know Why the Caged Bird Sings

The free bird leaps
on the back of the wind
and floats downstream
till the current ends
and dips his wings
in the orange sun rays
and dares to claim the sky.
But a bird that stalks
down his narrow cage
can seldom see through
his bars of rage
his wings are clipped and
his feet are tied
so, he opens his throat to sing.
The caged bird sings
with fearful trill
of the things unknown
but longed for still
and his tune is heard
on the distant hill
for the caged bird
sings of freedom
The free bird thinks of another breeze
and the trade winds soft through the sighing trees
and the fat worms waiting on a dawn-bright lawn
and he names the sky his own.
But a caged bird stands on the grave of dreams
his shadow shouts on a nightmare scream
his wings are clipped and his feet are tied
so, he opens his throat to sing
The caged bird sings
with a fearful trill
of things unknown
but longed for still
and his tune is heard
on the distant hill
for the caged bird
sings of freedom.

My final plea to all of you: let none of us be caged, rather, all of us completely free! Until we meet again. Take care, legends!

Afterword

I am prepared to evolve. The question is: Are you?

—Mother Nature

I HOPE YOU'VE enjoyed the unpacking of my lunch box, and I hope it has inspired you to move forward, thinking about what you're going to put in yours starting tomorrow. The best case scenario is you're prepared to move forward and start making some dynamic changes in your life. It only gets better from here.

As you walk into your life tomorrow, things are, no doubt, going to go wrong. Something will happen that will leave you feeling like the universe is kicking you down. Don't give this too much attention. Great things take time. You aren't suddenly going to be moving ahead at light speed without any interruptions; that's not the way life unfolds. It would be a mistake to assume that you've now read this book, you've selected the items you want in your lunch box, and now life is just going to be peachy. Don't make that grave assumption. Life is going to happen, my friends, and when it does, sometimes, it's going to knock you down. But remember, life doesn't knock us down for the purpose of hurting us; it knocks us down to give us the gift of understanding and humility.

Things will continue to get better, however. Your responsibility now is to find your purpose and passion for life. Make a plan to live that purpose and passion and then let the universe intercede on your behalf. It would be very wise to prepare for how you will react, respond, and move forward anytime adversity confronts your life. Don't ever forget that you are on your journey, not some other person's journey. The steps that you take and the progress that you make is up to you. Find a pace that is comfortable for you so that you can move forward with as much ease as possible. At the end of the day, the best thing you can do, is just do something to start moving your life in the direction that you want it to go.

Along the way, there will be naysayers. They won't necessarily understand why you are doing what you are doing, and that's okay. One of the biggest lessons I've learned recently from reading *Think Like a Monk* by Jay Shetty is: "People can't understand you because they struggle to understand themselves. They can't support you following your passion because they never followed theirs. No one gave them the opportunity to do that, and so they don't know how to give you the opportunity to do that. Don't expect it." Set your intentions, map out how you're going to get there, and then simply move forward in the direction you want to travel. If people discourage you along the way, don't buy into it. Your life is not their responsibility and vice versa.

When I first started writing this book roughly three years ago, trust me, my ego checked on me regularly; it was there to discourage me. It told me all sorts of things to keep me down. It posed questions like: Are you sure you're good enough to be a writer? Why would people want to hear what you have to say? It also found time to make bold statements like: "Nobody is going to read this because nobody knows or cares who you are." Guess what, it was hard at first, but I simply stopped listening. I decided instead to follow my heart and passion. I followed my instinct that my experiences and, thereby, the lessons I learned from them are valuable, and if those lessons can help just one person, then that is more than enough.

Writing this first book has been an incredibly therapeutic process for my soul. It's helped me relieve myself of many of the remnants of false beliefs that I still held inside. It's given me solace during the ups and downs of daily life. It's also inspired me to continue writing, no matter what happens to those writings.

This won't be my last book; I can guarantee that. I've loved the process so much and loved exploring my biggest passion: writing. The way I see it, this book has thirteen chapters. I can already envision that each chapter will eventually become its own individual book to form a sort of legends series. I hope you come along with me for the ride as we continue to evolve together and create a better life for everyone that centers around increased consciousness, compassion, and healing planet Earth.

Thank you so much for taking the time to read this book and stay tuned for more incredible things to come in the future from me and the Lunchbox Legends brand!

About the Author

T. J. ABNEY has been a writer, educator, and thought leader in the beauty industry for over a decade. In his professional role, he has spent the last thirteen years traveling the globe working alongside, developing and inspiring hairdressers from all walks of life. His upbringing and the broad experiences gained throughout his career, along with some tough life lessons, have given him a unique and heartfelt perspective on how to create the life that you desire.

T. J. has held a passion for writing for many years and is dedicated to helping others succeed in their life journey through his writings. Currently living in Phoenix, Arizona, he spends a majority of his time reading, writing, and hiking while maintaining a commitment to meditation, healthy food, fitness, and continuously looking within to search for the higher meanings in life.

Most recently, he founded the Lunchbox Legends brand where he strives to continue raising the consciousness and compassion of the human spirit daily through his monthly Tim Talks and through various inspirational and motivational methods. As a teacher at heart, T. J. continues to pursue opportunities through personal experiences that inspire others to reach for the absolute best in life every single day.

In his debut book, T. J. presents a comprehensive overview of how you can pack your lunch box for the life you want to experience through daily practice, utilizing the essential tools he has provided. Looking ahead, he plans to develop additional resources that take a deeper dive into each topic in this book where he can share more in-depth life stories, the individual lessons learned from each experience, and more significantly, to share those lessons to inspire others. You can become a part of his Lunch-Boxer tribe by following him on Instagram (lunchbox.legend), on Facebook (Lunchbox Legends), and on YouTube (Lunchbox Legends). You can also register on his website at www.lunchboxlegends.com to become an official Lunch-Boxer and to take part in everything on offer from the Lunchbox Legends brand.

CPSIA information can be obtained
at www.ICGtesting.com
Printed in the USA
BVHW072238281221
625049BV00003B/460